SPIRITUAL
identity

SPIRITUAL identity

BELIEVE GOD'S REVOLUTIONARY TRUTH

by Larry V. Silver

SPIRITUAL identity

Spiritual Identity: Believe God's Revolutionary Truth

Cover design by Pixels Logo Design

Interior design by www.bookclaw.com

Published in the United States of America

ISBN: 8-978-0-9787652-7-9

This book is dedicated to all who are searching for their spiritual identity.
(Galatians 2:20)

Acknowledgments

I sincerely want to thank the Lord Jesus Christ for allowing me to be His child and to walk with Him since my youth. This book is mainly about Him, but also about the people whom He loves. If He can transform me, He can transform anyone, given the opportunity. It is clear that we all need help, and in my life, the Lord provided Don Bartel as a mentor and friend. Don is living proof that it is not necessary to spend countless hours in order to have a positive impact on someone for eternity. Don was at the right place and the right time for me, beginning with his ministry to college students before I was even a believer.

From the time we met in 1982, Don has always given me the benefit of the doubt (which says a lot for him, if you know what I have been through). He is the godliest person and the most progressive thinker I know. Without his influence, this book would not have been written. I thank Don, along with David Needham (author of *Birthright*), for their review of the manuscript and their expert feedback.

Thanks to my twin brother, Dr. Dave Silver, for his encouragement and for refuting some of my questionable understanding—because iron sharpens iron—and for his input on this manuscript.

Thanks to Carole Davenport (Love Gifts Ministries International) for her exemplary walk, ministry, and online care of so many people around the world in Jesus, and for her willingness to offer insights on this manuscript, as well.

And finally, my thanks to Heidi Nigro, an accomplished writer and my first editor on this project, who was an answer to prayer. I am grateful for her spiritual maturity and needed input in polishing the text before it was sent to the publisher.

Table of Contents

Foreword

Years ago someone graciously sent me this story. There was a British cat named Rupert. He lived in a London suburb with a family named Robinson.

Rupert, it seems, had a habit of disappearing for a day or two, sometimes three. Then he would come back as though he had never left. One day Rupert appeared with a brand new collar. A bit suspicious, the Robinsons attached a note to the collar which said, "My name is Rubert. I live at 22 Lansdowne Place with the Robinsons." Then they waited. Soon Rupert vanished again. This time when he finally returned, another note was attached to his collar.

"At 84 Bington Road, where I live with the Cromwells, my name is Blackie." Someone heard about the British cat named Rupert and said, "That's a smart cat. He had the best of two worlds." But a lady older and wiser said, "Not so smart. He didn't know who he was and where he really belonged."

For an animal, such a confused identity is nothing to be too concerned about, but for a blood-bought Christian to be mistakenly torn between two identities is nothing short of a full-fledged tragedy.

Yet this very tragedy is widespread among God's people. Was a dual identity in Jesus' mind when He prayed "they are not of this world even as I am not of this world"? Has God actually "qualified us to share in the inheritance of the saints in light"? If He has, if you were suddenly separated from your physical body, would you—as you now are—fit in a holy heaven the very next moment?

Commonly, when a person behaves out of character, we say, "He is not himself today." Could the miracle of the new birth be great enough to justify our saying that whenever a Christian sins, that he is behaving "out of character"? Happily, this new birth miracle brings with it not only a radical change in identity but also all the resources necessary "for life and godliness."

In an effort to clarify this new covenant message, Larry Silver has produced this book. Each of its pages will encourage you to let the Scriptures speak for themselves without those well-intentioned often taught rationalizations which minimize the greatness of this new birth miracle. It is the earnest hope of the author that this book will have a positive effect not only in the lives of new believers but also among mature believers, as they take a refreshing look at God's revolutionary truth.

I share his hope that you will come away from your reading, both amazed and grateful for your glorious Lord Who by grace alone has made you His "by birth" child. So please read on!

David C. Needham, Professor Emeritus,
Multnomah Bible College

Introduction

Of making many books there is no end – Ecclesiastes 12:12.

I always thought this verse referred to how many books could be made, not to the book-writing process itself. Now, having had the challenging experience of putting together my own book, this verse has new meaning.

I felt compelled to put into writing what God and many brothers and sisters have taught me concerning the fascinating topic of spiritual identity.

What is spiritual identity? It is the biblical truth that God dwells in us through the Spirit of Jesus Christ, and through that indwelling, He is able to change us from the inside out. This God indwelling and Spirit filling work to fully carry out the purpose and meaning of life that God designed for us.

As believers, our fundamental nature is identified with God and His Spirit. Therefore, it should not surprise us that God identifies us with spiritual words and phrases that we would not normally apply to ourselves. Our spiritual identity, by grace, is now wrapped up in God's very person.

Though I do not consider myself to be a gifted writer, the biblical concept of spiritual identity and its implications have impacted me with such life-changing force that I have been compelled to share them with others. They have taken my mind and spirit higher than the heavens and seated me with the Lord of glory,

Jesus of Nazareth, and I do not believe that I have ever fully come back down to earth. Outward circumstances have not been able to penetrate Christ's take-over of my heart, though many things, people, and circumstances have tried.

I have invested many years reading, listening to, studying, testing, praying, memorizing, and meditating on God's Word and in fellowship with Him. Over this time, I have found that God has no problem speaking through His Holy Word. It says things about Christians that are so glorious and mind-boggling that, at some point, the spiritual seeker must wrestle with the question—do I believe all this or not?

For me, a young man from a Jewish upbringing, the answer to this question was neither expedient nor easy, but the truth was plastered all over the road to God. It turns out that a relationship with Him is the goal and the destination. Who would have guessed? And that relationship has every answer to every question we need to know this side of eternity. Not just ethereal, idealistic questions about man's existence, but practical questions of how to live a life of power and love.

Before receiving Jesus into my life, I was like Matt Damon in *The Bourne Identity*, face down in the ocean, left for dead, totally unaware of who I really was. Then Jesus revealed Himself, and through Him, my true spiritual identity began to take shape.

Spiritual Identity contains 24 characteristics of who Christ is in us through the power of a Spirit-regenerated life. Each characteristic is a wonder, a promise, a God-view, an infinite truth, an irrefutable foundation for the believer.

By taking each characteristic in its given order, we can build layer upon layer of truth. I encourage you to study each chapter carefully, prayerfully, and with a studied fellowship of like-hearted souls.

Who Are You?

For me, this revelation—who God says we are in Christ and who Christ is in us—started in the late 1980s, when I was at a conference with my mentor, Don Bartel, a leader for the Navigators, a worldwide Christian ministry dedicated to reaching God seekers and discipling them into spiritual maturity.

I openly shared with Don that I did not think I was doing well in my faith and that I felt like a "pride ball." He bantered back that he saw Christ in me and that I was viewing myself according to the flesh, not the Spirit. Then Don encouraged me to read David Needham's book, *Birthright,* a theological approach to spiritual identity that changed my life. He helped me see that the New Testament's view of believers is based on the truth of God's Word, not our self-perception.

Books can influence our thinking in very positive ways. My hope and prayer are that this book, like *Birthright* in my own life, will do that for you. I hope that it will clarify what the New Testament clearly teaches—that as believers in Jesus, we have a spiritual identity that is secure and wrapped in God's promises.

Because God is a spirit being, we who are created in His image, are also spirit beings. This doesn't mean that we don't have bodies (clearly, we do, and one day, the Bible teaches, we will receive new, perfect bodies suited for eternity with Him—1 Corinthians. 15:50–54), but for now, our earthly bodies are mere "tents" to house the "real us," which are eternal spirits, inseparably linked with Christ.

The truth about our spiritual identity in Christ is not contained in one verse or another, but due to its beauty and complexity is interwoven throughout the New Testament.

This book is meant to pull all of the pieces together so you can see the brilliance of the diamond formed from the heat and pressure of God's Word.

Each chapter of *Spiritual Identity* is purposed to view this diamond from a different facet. My hope is that the sparkle will be so glorious that it will permanently encourage your inner man and catapult you to where you belong – seated with your Savior in the heavenlies. If I help you to achieve a more solid spiritual identity and encourage you to be stronger and bolder in your faith, my investment will have been worth it.

Ultimately, my goal is to increase awareness among believers of New Testament concepts and principles that have made the church great. If believers can be who God created them to be, they will do the things He is calling them to do. Then the world will know that the Father sent the Son.

What a privilege!

Larry

www.larryvsilver.com

1

mirror, mirror on the wall

Do you know who you are? This is the question that man has struggled with throughout the ages. Most people would answer by giving their names, their ages, what they do, where they live and work, and their favorite roles: husband, wife, son, significant other, grandparent.

Some Christians will even expound on what they believe, where they are going in life, and their desire for others to follow suit. But is this how God sees us?

The answer to this question is important because, as Christians, we are tasked with bringing the light of Christ into a dark world. But what happens when the lives of believers look just like those of unbelievers?

Have you really thought about this question? Just look around you. Christians and unbelievers have similar divorce and crime rates, business ethics, and lifestyles. What kind of impact is our Christian testimony having? Very little—if any. The unbelieving world sees that our belief and faith in Christ doesn't change our thoughts and behavior in a practical sense. Yes, it may lift our spirits on Sunday and give us hope for eternal life, but then, so do other religions. Overall, the world is not impressed. Can you blame them? For a long time, I was among them.

My Story

I suffered from an identity crisis right from birth. Born an identical twin in a Jewish family in Overbrook Park, Philadelphia, I struggled to know who I was, the purpose of life, and my part in it.

The conservative synagogue my family attended was just a few doors from my home on the same side of the street. Although I was intrigued by the Old Testament stories and knew that the Jews were God's chosen people, I did not know what we were chosen for. I had heard about a coming Messiah from time to time. There were so many things that we (the Jews) needed to be delivered from. But my understanding did not go very deep.

It's not as if I didn't try to understand. At the ripe old age of six, there was a gorge down the street where I used to go to seek God. The neighborhood lore was that a bridge used to run over the gorge, but it collapsed while cars were traveling over it. The fact that there were tires and car parts down the steep sides of the gorge seemed to confirm this horrifying tale. Although I was afraid to be there, I thought God would be in this sacred place, so I would go there and ask Him questions that my parents and others could not seem to answer.

When I turned eight, my family moved from Pennsylvania to New Jersey. We blended nicely with the natives (the Gentiles) in our new neighborhood. After a year or two, my parents no longer required that we attend synagogue. When I turned 13, my grandmother died and even the thought of a Bar Mitzvah faded. Religion and tradition stopped being a priority in our household.

During my high school years, my parent's relationship went downhill. By my senior year, they were separated, never to join together again. Senior year was a time of regression. I experimented with drugs and alcohol. I joined a rock band, playing the drums. Dave, my twin, played the guitar. It was a time of independence and rebellion, but our upbringing prevented us from getting into any major trouble.

Although my three brothers and I did well academically, I entered my freshman year at LaSalle College (now a university) disillusioned with life. Satan loves disillusion, as it offers a chance for him to lure people away from the truth. Though the glamour of drugs and alcohol had worn off, I now sought meaningful communication with anyone who was willing to talk about life. The first person I found was John, a fellow freshman who lived on the same floor I did.

Like me, he preferred talking late into the night over drinking or drugs. After his gay tendencies revealed themselves, however, I sought a counselor instead.

In my counseling sessions, I discoursed frequently about death. This alarmed my counselor and she brought in a psychologist. He didn't see me as suicidal but acknowledged that I was grappling with some legitimate questions about life. Neither he nor the counselor, however, could provide satisfying answers.

For some extra money, I took a job on weekends as a mobile disc jockey. I enjoyed the music, dancing, and emcee role, showing people a fun time. In between classes and homework, I would relax in the music room. Bernard, the janitor, showed an unusual interest in me. We quickly became friends. Shortly thereafter, I took up video arcade games, and Bernard would supply me with quarters. He seemed to have an endless supply, which, at the time, I never questioned.

One day, he asked me what my license plate number was and proceeded to announce that my number would win the lottery. The next day, he nonchalantly tossed me the paper. Can you guess what the winning number was?

Bernard, it seemed, had psychic powers. He even claimed that he could cause me to think about him, even call him. Often when I called, he would exclaim that I had just done his bidding. Whenever I tried to find where he lived, I was unable.

Years later, when I attempted to find Bernard, there was no record that he ever worked for the college. It turns out, I didn't need to find him. Even though I had moved so many times that my parents had trouble keeping track of me, whenever I least expected it, Bernard would appear.

Who was this mysterious person and why did he show up in my life at that time? I realized later that, by distracting me from my spiritual quest through appealing alternatives, Bernard was one of Satan's decoys to keep me from the truth.

By the end of my freshman year, a girl from my hometown in New Jersey was showing interest in a serious relationship. I went along for the ride. We got an apartment together 30 minutes from my college. I attempted to commute my second year but saddled with a dysfunctional relationship, I soon dropped out of LaSalle, even though I was just shy of a 3.6 GPA.

Now I was responsible for taking care of the two of us. I landed a job selling family portraits for straight commission and began to travel from store to store and invest 10 days per stint in each new place. Being on the road quickly revealed that my girlfriend was interested in whoever happened to be around at the moment. Soon, that person wasn't me.

Again on my own, my work had become traveling photo salesman by default. I would meet hundreds of people every day in the food and department stores I was assigned to. I enjoyed the challenge of selling, but there were many lonely days when there was no friend with whom to talk.

In early 1982, during a photo promotion in Reading, Pennsylvania, a couple came into the store and promptly bought some family portraits. After I secured their five dollar deposit, they began to question me. The first thing I found surprising was that they asked my name. No customer had ever asked before. Then they asked me about my background. When they heard that I was Jewish, they seemed excited. I told them that I was pretty streetwise.

I noticed right away that there was something different about them. The comment just flowed out unexpectedly. "I see something in the two of you that I have never seen before. What is it?" They chuckled, joyfully acknowledging that what I had just said was true indeed. Instead of answering directly, they continued their line of questioning.

"What is the hope of a Jewish person?" they asked. I replied, "I don't know. I believe in God and I try to be the best person that I can be." "From our understanding of the Jewish scriptures, it seems as though Israel was waiting for the Messiah." "Well, I don't read those anymore. Though, I still remember some stories from Hebrew School." I looked at them intently. "You are going to tell me that you think Jesus Christ is the Messiah." They laughed, incredulous at how fast I read them. "I told you that I've been on the streets for a while. I don't believe that stuff about Jesus. If you want to, that's up to you."

They excused themselves and promised to come back later that day. They had something they wanted to show me. Upon their return, they presented a chart showing all the major world religions. The heading stated something like, "The Truth of Being Born Again and the Error of All Other Religions." I remember thinking how audacious that title seemed to me. I also remember the man pointing his finger at me in a strong way (I did not like when anyone did that) and challenging me.

"Larry," he said. "I challenge you. Just pray to your God, the God of Abraham, Isaac, and Jacob, and just ask Him if Jesus is the Jewish Messiah. If he's not, you have nothing to lose. But if he is…"

Never again was I to see this couple or even remember their names. If only they knew the events that were soon to occur in my life.

That night, I returned to my rundown motel. A bar was attached to the side and I was having a beer, wondering which gal I might pick up. One was showing interest from a distance, but somehow, I was too bothered about the events of the day to pursue it. That couple had gotten through a chink in my armor. In disgust, I left the beer and the gal where they were.

Back in the room, I tossed and turned. Restless, I turned on the TV. The first words I heard were from Pat Robertson of the 700 Club. "I know some of you Jews are watching tonight." I turned around to see who was in the room with me. "The Bible says that you are a stubborn and stiff-necked people. You always demand miraculous signs." He flashed scriptures on to the screen from the Old Testament to prove his point.

Then he did something that I will never forget. He pointed his big, bony finger at the viewing audience and said the very same words I'd heard earlier in the day. "I challenge you Jews who are watching. Just pray to your God, the God of Abraham, Isaac, and Jacob, and ask Him whether Jesus is the Jewish Messiah. What do you have to lose?"

Well! Two Gentiles had challenged me on the same day about some Jesus who they claimed was raised from the dead. Until now, the only times I had heard Jesus' name were when someone from the old neighborhood hit their finger with a hammer! Now there were two boney fingers both pointing at me to pray.

Years earlier, I had asked God for answers about life, but I had never heard anything back. Still, I did believe in God. I had always believed in God since I could remember.

I prayed out loud for the first time in my life. "God, I'm a Jew, I don't believe in Jesus, but if He is really alive like these Gentiles are saying to me, then I will put my faith in Him. If He's alive, then it should not be too difficult for him to reveal Himself to me. You know, since we Jews always demand miraculous signs." (I was still upset about Pat's comment.) "Come to me and show Yourself to me and I will believe in You and commit myself to You."

After putting the onus back on God, I easily fell back asleep. After all, it wasn't my problem anymore. The next day as I was in the shower, hair lathered, I heard a voice. Not audibly, but in my mind. I had never had this experience before.

"I have come in answer to your prayers," it said. The voice was so clear that I did not even finish rinsing the shampoo out of my hair. I put a towel around me and went, shivering, out into the room. In the bathroom, there was a shower and toilet. Outside was a foyer with a double sink. My hairdryer had been plugged into the big mirror's outlet for all five days I had been there.

The room was pitch dark. I sat on one of the double beds closest to the bathroom. Then asked out loud, "How did you come in answer to my prayers?"

The voice spoke again. "What you are looking for is on the mirror." "The mirror… ?"

I stood up and flicked on the light. I was stunned to see symbols scratched into the glass of the mirror. They did not spell anything or mean anything in English. They looked Greek to me.

The next thing I knew, the clerk and the motel manager were trying to calm me down as I attempted to ascertain where the letters had come from. They assured me that the writing had not been there when I moved in. Terrified, I asked for another room, but there were none available. For the next five days, I continued to stare at the symbols, wondering how they got there.

I called my mother and twin brother to tell them of the bizarre incident. Dwayne, my brother's college roommate, seemed to affirm that God was revealing something to me, but it all seemed too weird and farfetched to me.

This event did not convert me, but it did get me to investigate the New Testament for myself. "I don't trust any Christians as far as I can throw them," I would mutter as I read the enthralling stories in a book I never had reason to look at before.

Very quickly, I became enamored with Christ. He was like a superhero. In fact, reading the New Testament was more like reading a comic book than a religious book. How could Jesus live like that? Always doing good and overcoming the odds? I even called each of my parents and asked them why I had not learned of this Jewish rabbi before.

What didn't they tell me about him? I needed to have Christians challenge me to look into it. I even told my mom about the mirror incident. I wondered what she thought of her nice unstable Jewish boy.

One day, I read in the gospels the story of Jesus visiting his hometown and how they were taken aback and offended. After all, He grew up with them. They were so angry that they intended to throw him over the cliff on which the town was built. The sentence ended at the bottom of the right-hand page.

I turned the page in suspense and read, "He walked right through the crowd and went on His way." I kept flipping back and forth to see if I was perhaps missing a page. I was not. How could Jesus walk through a mob of one thousand angry Jews? I have personally seen a single Orthodox Jew clear out a whole New York City subway train because one of the passengers provoked him. Now here was Jesus walking right through their midst. He must be God, I thought. I felt afraid of what that might mean.

During the time of my reading the New Testament, I visited my brother at his university. His roommate, Dwayne, turned out to be a Christian. He shared a very clear explanation of God's plan for mankind and how Jesus, being the Messiah had completed the work on the cross, dying for my sins. He drew out a bridge with God on one side and man on the other.

"Which side are you on?" he asked.

"Man's side. Which side are you on?"

"God's."

"Well, how do I get over there?"

Dwayne shared John 1:12: "Yet to all those who had received Him, to those who believed in His name, He gave the right to become children of God."

I told Dwayne that I had already done that on my own. He then shared 1 John 5:11–13. This passage talked about knowing for sure that I had eternal life. As he was still sharing with me, I bowed my head in response to the challenge to know for sure that I was going to heaven and that I was saved right now. The date: November 15, 1982. I was 19 years old. Over time, I learned that the symbols scratched on my mirror in Reading, Pennsylvania, were the Greek symbols of the Alpha and Omega.

> *I was in the Spirit on the Lord's Day and heard behind me a great voice, as of a trumpet, saying, I am Alpha and Omega, the First and the Last: and what thou seest, write in a book, and send it unto the seven churches which are in Asia. (Revelation 1:10,11, kjv)*

It became clear to me that Jesus had come in answer to the prayer of this stubborn and stiff-necked Jew. It is interesting to note that the voice that accompanied the symbols was, in fact, Jesus Himself and that He was alive. Was it possible that I could now find my true identity in Jesus Christ?

Some have asked me how I know that it was Jesus, not Satan, who engraved the symbols on the mirror that day. My response begins with a bit of sarcasm. "Thank you, Satan, for doing such a thing—for getting me to read the Bible and helping me get to know the Jewish Messiah."

My point is clear. Satan does not lead people to Jesus. I know Satan as a deceiver who loves to promote fear, pride, and confusion. He loves to mimic God and to try to steal His praise, honor, and glory. If he did write the message in an attempt to lead me away from Jesus, he made a whopper of a miscalculation!

Within a day or two of praying with Dwayne, I approached David, my twin brother.

"Dave, you know how God has always been obvious to us..."

"Yes," he said with hesitation.

"Well, now Jesus is obvious to us."

Within one week, David came to the Jewish Messiah. Now we are eternal twins instead of just earthly twins. Now we are laboring together to help one another find our identity in Him.

Though I was unworthy, undeserving, and not outwardly seeking at the time, God chose to reveal something about Himself to me. It also changed my relationship with mirrors forever.

I had always been uncomfortable looking at myself in the mirror. I did not know who I was as a person, nor my meaning and purpose in life. It's challenging enough to be a twin, but even if you are not, how do you look confidently in the mirror every morning, ready to tackle God's plan for your life? Now, for the first time, I could. I knew what my life was about. It was living for God, to accept who He had made me to be, and to appreciate the special uniqueness that He created in me for such a time as this—to serve Him.

Since then, God has shown me many things about who we as believers are in Christ. Listen to these passages and relate them to my story and to yours.

> *For if any be a hearer of the word, and not a doer, he is like unto a man beholding his natural face in a glass [mirror]: For he beholdeth himself, and goeth his way, and straightway forgetteth what manner of man he was. (James 1:23,24 kjv)*

> *Now the Lord is that Spirit: and where the Spirit of the Lord is, there is liberty. But we all, with open face beholding as in a glass [mirror] the glory of the Lord, are changed into the same image from glory to glory, even as by the Spirit of the Lord. (2 Corinthians 3:17,18 kjv)*

Through the mirror of scripture, I have found that which I had been seeking my whole life—my identity.

Pilgrim's Mirror

A story in Pilgrim's Progress summarizes the impact the "mirror of identity" can make in the life of a person who is open to seeing life from God's vantage point.

> "Now when the Shepherds had shown them all these things, they took them back to the palace and entertained them with what the house had to offer. Mercy, being young and expecting a child, longed for something she saw there, but she was ashamed to ask. Her mother-in-law then asked her what ailed her, for she looked like an individual not well."

Then Mercy said, "I can't take my mind off a mirror that hangs in the dining room. If I can't have it, I think I'll miscarry." Then her mother-in-law said, "I'll mention your desire to the Shepherds, and they won't deny you of it."

"But I am ashamed that these men should know how I longed," said Mercy.

"No, my daughter," said Christiana. "It's no shame but a virtue to long for such a thing as that."

So Mercy said, "Then, Mother, if you please, ask the Shepherds if they're willing to sell it."

Now the Mirror was one in a thousand. It would present a person one way with one's own features exactly, but turn it another way and it should show the actual face and similitude of the Prince of Pilgrims himself. Yes, I have talked with them who know, and they have said that by looking through the Mirror they have seen the actual Thorn of Crowns upon His head. They have also seen in it the holes in His hands, in His feet, and in His side. Certainly, there is such an excellency in that Mirror that it will show Him to an individual wherever the person would like to see Him, whether living or dead, whether in earth or heaven, whether in a state of humiliation or in His exaltation, and whether coming to suffer or coming to reign.[1]

As we seek our spiritual identities, we will learn more about reigning as kings and priests in Christ's name, suffering with others, and exalting in the position we have in the heavenly realm. The position described in the New Testament is so glorious that the revealed truths can be misconstrued and misunderstood in ways not intended by scripture.

For this reason, before I launch into the discussion about OUR spiritual identity, which is the purpose of this book, I want to clear the decks about who God is and also recognizing who we are not!

2

who you are not

Before we discuss all the wonderful and glorious things that the Bible says about us as believers in Jesus, it is important that we clearly establish who we are not, both individually and corporately.

First and most importantly, we are not God! Listening to followers of the New Age movement, it might sound as if we are. But the scriptures (not to mention earthly reality) reveal that we are not.

One of the best illustrations of this can be found in the Book of Job, which tells the story of how God allowed Job to be tested by Satan. With God's permission, Satan took away Job's family, his livelihood, his health—even his respect. Left with only his wife and a broken spirit, Job lifted up his lament to God.

To his complaint, God replied:

> *Where were you when I laid the earth's foundation?*
>
> *Tell me, if you understand. Who marked off its dimensions? Surely you know! Who stretched a measuring line across it? On what were its footings set, or who laid its cornerstone—while the morning stars sang together and all the angels shouted for joy?*
>
> *Who shut up the sea behind doors when it burst forth from the womb, when I made the clouds its garment and wrapped it in thick darkness, when I fixed limits*

for it and set its doors and bars in place, when I said, "This far you may come and no farther; here is where your proud waves halt?"

Have you ever given orders to the morning, or shown the dawn its place, that it might take the earth by the edges and shake the wicked out of it?...

Have you journeyed to the springs of the sea or walked in the recesses of the deep? Have the gates of death been shown to you? Have you seen the gates of the shadow of death? Have you comprehended the vast expanses of the earth? Tell me, if you know all this.

What is the way to the abode of light? And where does darkness reside? Can you take them to their places? Do you know the paths to their dwellings?

Surely you know, for you were already born! You have lived so many years! (Job 38:4–13, 16–21)

God has much more to say to Job, and at the end, Job's response is abject humility. He says, "I spoke once, but I have no answer—twice, but I will say no more" (Job 40:5).

God is the Creator. He is the Alpha and the Omega. He was and is and is to come. He is the Almighty. All the "omnis" describe Him: omnipotent (all powerful), omniscient (all-knowing), and omnipresent (all present). God is worthy of all praise, honor, and glory. God is love. His person radiates goodness to all His creation. God is holy.

His perfect nature and character are never changing. But God is also just. Because of His sinless nature, God fights against sin, evil, and anything that sets itself up in place of or against Him. Hopefully, we will never think that we are (or could be) God. In his pride, this is what Satan does, and we don't want to be like Satan. Still, we do sometimes rebel against God's sovereignty or think we have a better way of doing things. When this happens to you, try reading the full text of Job 38–41.

It is necessary to establish our limitations right at the beginning of our discussion. Why is this so important? Because the truth about our spiritual identity is so uplifting that, if not seen in its proper context, it could be misconstrued. God says wonderful things about us, but we have to remember that we are still His creation.

Grasping by the Spirit

The Word of God is clear about our identity, but these spiritually-charged truths are difficult for the natural mind to grasp.

> *The man without the Spirit does not accept the things that come from the Spirit of God, for they are foolishness to him, and he cannot understand them, because they are spiritually discerned. (1 Corinthians 2:14)*

Fortunately, as believers in Christ, we have the Spirit of God in us, willing and working to accomplish God's will. The Spirit is capable of helping us understand these truths, and when we believe them, He gains ground to move forward and "do His thing."

But beware! When God shows up in the person of the Holy Spirit, He does not come to take sides. He comes to take over!

This is clearly seen in Joshua 5:13-15 when Joshua asks, "Are you for us or for our enemies?" "Neither," he replied, "but as commander of the army of the Lord I have now come." When Joshua senses whose presence he is in, he hits the ground. This should be our natural response to God, as well—to keep our hearts humble, submissive, and open to His marching orders.

We are altogether different from our Maker. We are made of temporal stuff in these bodies of flesh. He is the eternal "I AM." God is what He is, regardless of time, space, and circumstances. He is a sovereign being, in control of everything. Fortunately for us, He loves His creation and desires to co-labor with us for His purposes and will.

This co-laboring can only occur if we belong to God, and we belong to God only if we receive the person of Christ into our hearts and live by faith. It is God who gives us the gift of faith so that no person can boast before Him, but we still need to respond and offer repentance for a life that is "off the mark" of God's glory.

Missing the Mark

What do I mean by "off the mark"? It's another way of talking about sin. When translated, the word "sin" means "missing the mark." In ancient days, an archer would practice his trade by aiming at a target some distance away. Usually, an aid would be close by to help. When the arrows completely missed the target, the apprentice would shout, "sin!" This meant that the arrows had not even nicked the target, let alone hit the bulls-eye.

Our sin causes us to miss God's purpose for our lives. However, as believers, His Spirit is given to us as a helper of our hearts, and the Spirit diligently reaches out to guide us in all things.

It is all too easy to fall back into the patterns in which we once lived when we were apart from Christ. When this happens, we are not allowing the regenerating work of the Spirit to have His way. It is a matter of who is in control. Is it us? or God? Jesus desires to be Lord of our lives, and as we grow up in our faith, we clearly see that His Lordship makes a tremendous difference. It is a matter of our inner man being impacted by the Lord's Spirit, thus constituting us from the inside out to be and do according to His pleasure.

If we are not constituted rightly before Him, our actions shoot way off course, just like the archer's arrows. In God's economy, hitting the bulls-eye is impossible through our own fleshly efforts. It is only after He fundamentally changes who we are that we can begin to hit the mark, and yes, even the bulls-eye of our lives.

Prayerfully approach the following passage from the book of Ephesians. As you read, resist any inclination to understand the verse based on your past. Renounce anything that you have learned from man and let the Spirit illuminate your mind. As it is written, "they will all be taught by God" (John 6:45).

> *And you hath he quickened, who were dead in trespasses and sins; Wherein in time past ye walked according to the course of this world, according to the*

prince of the power of the air, the spirit that now worketh in the children of disobedience: Among whom also we all had our conversation in times past in the lusts of our flesh and of the mind; and were by nature the children of wrath, even as others. (Ephesians 2:1–3, kjv)

What a bleak existence we had before our regeneration by the Holy Spirit! Go back and consider this passage again. Notice that before the point of God's regeneration in our hearts, we were by nature objects of His anger. God is holy, and we were off the mark. Not just our actions, but our whole being was out of tune with Him. We were on Satan's frequency. Without God, Satan had a direct dial-up connection to our souls.

Computer geeks might very well call this GIGO—Garbage In, Garbage Out. We put garbage in and garbage comes out. Apart from God, even our best and kindest deeds are as "filthy rags" in God's sight (Isaiah 64:6). This was God's way of telling His chosen ones, the Jews, that their best human efforts at righteousness were like a woman's monthly menstrual pad. What a mental picture! God is not impressed by our human efforts apart from His transforming power.

Receive Something Different

To be transformed, we must first receive something different than we had as unbelievers. As unbelievers, we were sinful. It was our very nature and heart to do wrong and to choose evil apart from faith birthed in God.

The LORD saw how great man's wickedness on the earth had become, and that every inclination of the thoughts of his heart was only evil all the time. The LORD was grieved that he had made man on the earth, and his heart was filled with pain. So the LORD said, "I will wipe mankind, whom I have created, from the face of the earth – men and animals, and creatures that move along the ground, and birds of the air – for I am grieved that I have made them." (Genesis 6:5–7)

But our nature changes when we receive Jesus. When Jesus died on the cross, He took the punishment and wrath of God for us. When we receive Him into our hearts by faith, we no longer have to fear God's fiery punishment. Rather, God accepts the punishment that Jesus took in our stead.

We are forgiven and can stand blameless before Him. Not only this but at the moment of salvation, God fundamentally changes our spiritual identity. Instead of our old nature (the old man), whose natural instinct is to sin, He replaces it with a new nature (the new man) who, through the indwelling of the Holy Spirit, naturally desires to live for Him. God regenerates us through the Spirit and resets our spiritual programming to obey Him.

We must believe what God says in His Word or we will be duped by Satan's lie. What is this lie? That we are unable to please God, unable to walk by faith, and unable to do anything for Him. Satan tells us this in order to steal our confidence in who God's Word says we are and to severely inhibit, impede, and even abort our divine call and destiny.

But this is where the mystery and wonder of God can accomplish something that we could never accomplish on our own. Through God's transforming power, we can now shoot our arrows straight and sure. We can hit the mark. It takes faith in God's Word and revelation through it to accept this truth.

The Greatest News

Though I have spent the chapter telling you who we are not, this is not bad news. On the contrary, it is really the best news we can ask for. God loves us even more than we can imagine, and as part of His perfect plan for us, He decided to take up residence in the lives and hearts of those who believe the gospel—the good news of who Jesus is and why He came to the earth. The Holy Spirit came into our physical bodies—not to take sides, but to take over!

It is beyond comprehension that, in sending His Son to die on the cross, God decided to do a new thing and indwell anyone who believes the gospel. Now, it is His desire to walk with us in the most intimate setting, the human heart.

God's residence and home address is no longer just heaven, but wherever you live as a believer in Him. You could even say that your Father is living within you and you have become his child.

3

children of God

See what great love the Father has lavished on us, that we should be called children of God! And that is what we are! The reason the world does not know us is that it did not know Him. Dear friends, now we are children of God, and what we will be has not yet been made known. (1 John 3:1-2)

Yet to all who did receive Him, to those who believed in His name, He gave the right to become children of God. (John 1:12)

The Spirit himself testifies with our spirit that we are God's children. (Romans 8:16)

This is an awesome fact for the believer in Jesus. We are now God's children. Some feel that all people are God's children since we all descended from the same man, Adam. It is true that there is only one race, the human race, and we are all a part of it. But the Bible is clear that it is by faith in Jesus, and His atoning and sacrificial death on the Cross, that we have the right to now become His children. The verse just before Romans 8:16 says "…the Spirit you received brought about your adoption to sonship. And by Him, we cry, "Abba Father." God is no longer far off and distant; He is up close, personal, and caring.

Sons and Daughters

As a child of God, we are His sons and daughters. How do you feel about your children? Do you have unconditional love for them? Is there anything they can do to take away your love? Most parents would say no to that question.

Of course, we want them to do well with their lives. We want them to make wise decisions and to be happy, right? Should God be any different than human parents? It is instinctive for human parents, being made in God's image, to care for their children. This is part of our spiritual identity. This is part of our DNA, the fabric of who we are. We are children first, but then parents. As a parent, often there is a paradigm shift. All of a sudden, a parent experiences unconditional love for the child. It just comes as part of the parental DNA that God imbued.

He is our Heavenly Father, who does not change like a shifting shadow (James 1:17) but is a constant. Jesus Christ is the same yesterday, today, and forever (Hebrews 13:8). People may change, but God does not. This should be a comfort to you as life unfolds. He will forever be your Father. You will forever be His child. He accepts you in the beloved (Ephesians 1:6, kjv). Another way of saying this is that you are a child who is loved. God promises that He will never leave you and never forsake you (Hebrews 13:5).

He is a Father who is good and always wants what is best for you as His child. This is where trust comes in. Since God is good and has your best interests at heart, would it not be wise to trust Him at all times (Psalm 62:8) and in every situation?

If you reason out the above statement, it becomes clear that trusting God at all times is a logical choice and lifestyle. If only it were that easy, all of His children would be trusting Him and walking by faith. Unfortunately, reality shows otherwise. In our culture, there does not appear to be a big difference in the behavior of the believing child of God and the unbeliever. Both seem to be making their independent choices and using worldly criteria as priority ahead of God's Word.

If we really believed in the depths of our hearts that we are His children, then we could really trust in His goodness throughout life and in our decisions- big and small. God's Word declares us to be His children all over the New Testament. We are part of his family as soon as we enter this faith by believing in the gospel message.

John 1:12 makes it clear also that we are not just believing a message but receiving a person - Jesus Christ - into our hearts. We are allowing Him to come in by faith and to rule in our hearts through the promised Holy Spirit. It is not necessary to understand how all this works right away.

What is important is to believe that God is true, His Word is true, and He encourages every person to repent of their sin, believe the good news (of eternal life and salvation - John 5:24), and to begin their faith adventure placing God ahead of all priorities and things in one's life. Matthew 6:33 promises that if you do this, He will give you everything else in addition - your needs, wants, desires (Psalm 37:4 nasb), and imaginations (Ephesians 3:20).

Princes and Princesses

We are the apple of God's eye. We are His children. It is hard to fathom what we really mean to God, except that we can see the proof of His love by the death of His Son. Jesus died to bring us into His family forever. In another chapter, I discuss the verses that say we are made kings because of His blood. I think that some will have trouble believing this fact about themselves. But, it may be easier to believe that you are a child of God. In Revelation, it states that He is the King of Kings and the Lord of Lords (Revelation 17:14, 19:16).

If it is true that He is the King of Kings, and the Bible states it plainly, then as His child, you are now a prince or princess. You are royalty. You are part of the King's family. You are welcome at His table to dine and feast as your heart desires. Your thoughts matter to the King- your well being, and your happiness. It all matters to Him. What kind of father would not give his child everything he could for their well being? How much more the God of all spirits? He is the best Father imaginable.

Abba Father

The New Testament reveals that our spiritual status is children of God. God has become a daddy to us. When we pray, we are speaking as His son, His daughter, His child, to engage with His thoughts in our situation.

Realize that our Abba Father responds with love and compassion like our earthly dads respond when they hear us hurting.

Our Heavenly Father responds to our hurts and our tears with more concern and understanding then we can possibly fathom.

Our Future

In 1 John 3:2, it says that what we will be is not yet known. It is in conjunction with being God's child that this is stated. What potential does a prince or princess have in the kingdom of the King? The potential is unlimited. The implied power is there. The credentials are known. The family is preeminent. When you realize that your future is skewed by your Father toward the good, the prosperous, the successful, and the hopeful, it is very humbling. Our futures are very bright and full of possibilities.

> *"For I know the plans I have for you," says the Lord. "Plans to prosper you and not to harm you, plans to give you a hope and a future." (Jeremiah 29:11)*

Our spiritual identity begins with this concept of sonship, this truth that we are God's children. Please internalize it, receive its truth, and bask in your great standing in this short time you have to be part of the family whose Father is the greatest Father in the Universe.

By being part of this family of God, you have now gained an inheritance and become an heir.

4

heirs

Now if we are children, then we are heirs—heirs of God and co-heirs with Christ, if indeed we share in his sufferings in order that we may also share in his glory. (Romans 8:17)

That being justified by his grace, we should be made heirs according to the hope of eternal life. (Titus 3:7, kjv)

The Bible is clear that since we are children of God, we are now heirs of God and co-heirs with Christ. What an awesome thing to know as a believer about yourself. An heir means that you are going to inherit the property and estate of your guardian. It is a blessing, to say the very least, that God is our Father, and we are part of His family. The gospel has brought us by faith and through grace into this mighty inheritance.

There are neat promises about our inheritance that affirm and confirm the fact that we are now heirs. Ephesians 1:14 speaks of the Holy Spirit, "who is a deposit guaranteeing our inheritance until the redemption of those who are God's possession—to the praise of His glory." The indwelling Holy Spirit is a down payment of our future inheritance. It is guaranteed. When a person dies, the executor reads and executes their Last Will and Testament. In Jesus' Last Will and Testament, he is leaving everything to us. He entrusted the Father to be His Executor. Jesus' death and resurrection assured our position by faith for eternity.

In verse 18 of the same chapter, Paul drills down even further:

> "I pray that the eyes of your heart may be enlightened in order that you may know the hope to which he has called you, the riches of his glorious inheritance in his holy people."

We need spiritual light to see how God's riches are being poured out for us. First, we have the hope of eternal life through Christ.

Second, we have all of God's riches at our disposal to enjoy and to use for His glory forever. This is hard to comprehend, but it is true nonetheless. Your Father is the richest, the most generous tycoon in Heaven and on the earth. A portion of what God has is yours.

Colossians 3:24 confirms this truth. "[Y]ou know that you will receive an inheritance from the Lord as a reward. It is the Lord Christ you are serving." Our future inheritance reveals who we are serving and that a sure reward awaits us who trust in this promise. There is nothing wrong with living our best today in the knowledge that our actions will bring about a significant reward.

In the film, *The Ultimate Gift*, billionaire Red Stevens, played by James Garner dies at the beginning and challenges his grandson Jason to go through a series of steps to gain his inheritance. These 12 tasks are designed to equip him, to mature him, and to prove his worth for a portion of the inheritance. Jason nearly gives up several times during the movie, not realizing that every task he successfully completes, is building his wealth substantially.

At the finale of the film, Jason has been transformed by this arduous process, which initially strips him of any wealth and deals with his "entitlement mentality." When he chooses to donate the $100 million health complex that he has designed and built for a good cause, then he is entrusted with the real riches of the estate - billions of dollars.

In similar fashion, God is hoping that we will love fully in this world, though it is certain to be fraught with suffering and hardship, so he can lavish his riches on us for all eternity. I know that these riches will make Red Steven's billions look like petty cash (chump change) on that day.

Hebrews 9:15 declares that "For this reason, Christ is the mediator of a new covenant, that those who are called may receive the promised eternal inheritance—now that He has died as a ransom to set them free from the sins committed under the first covenant." We are free to serve God now in the way of the spirit. Our past sins are forgiven and cast far away. Our new life is fresh and vital to His Kingdom. Let's make it count.

1 Peter 1:4, kjv concludes the matter:

> *To an inheritance incorruptible, and undefiled, and that fadeth not away, reserved in heaven for you.*

Wow, we have a secure future. If we can wrap our arms and minds around that, it will supernaturally affect the present. Our spiritual identity as heirs will be a daily reality and we can risk the daily challenges that present themselves.

To be crystal clear, we, as believers, only have an inheritance because of who we are in Jesus. We are considered heirs with the Father and co-heirs with Christ. That is amazing and remarkable. It is mind-boggling, but since the Bible says it, we know it to be true. Just realize that we are not heirs because of our works or because of anything great in and of ourselves.

This is important because realizing all we have in Christ is what keeps our feet firmly planted on the ground. That knowledge keeps us out of danger and humble at all times. It is even important to realize that how we view and treat others can affect our daily life and have repercussions. Peter obviously had experience in his own marriage that was a spiritual revelation and caused him to be careful to keep his loved ones at the forefront of his mindset.

Here is what he sets forth in 1 Peter 3:7:

> *"Husbands, in the same way, be considerate as you live with your wives, and treat them with respect as the weaker partner and as heirs with you of the gracious gift of life so that nothing will hinder your prayers.*

Therefore, if husbands don't act in a considerate way or have respect for wives as they are, they will be negatively impacted.

The devil, you can be sure, will seize those opportunities to make you pay for ill-treatment of your spouse, your children, your parents, your siblings, and your spiritual family. So, please consider those around you and realize that they are very much joint heirs with you of eternal life, the gospel, and your great inheritance for eternity.

You are now part of a royal family that has its inheritance in Heaven forever. So the Bible makes it clear that you can reign on the earth now as kings in preparation for that inheritance.

5

kings

For thou wast slain, and hast redeemed us to God by thy blood out of every kindred, and tongue, and people, and nation; And hast made us unto our God kings and priests: and we shall reign on the earth. (Revelation 5:9,10 kjv)

It is one thing that the Lord loved us and cleansed us of all sin. It is quite another that we have been made kings. We now have royal blood flowing through our spiritual veins—the blood of Christ, the ruler of kings.

It is beyond understanding what the scripture says about this. But by faith, we must say, "Amen. Lord, I am a king." Otherwise, we deny the Word of our faith and call God a liar.

Isn't it ironic that, rather than accept our place of kingship, we would rather act unassuming and claim no such greatness for ourselves? But the Lord is the reason that we are kings. It is not of ourselves. We have been made kings by the royal and effective blood of the Lamb.

The Apostle Paul appealed in 1 Corinthians 4:8, saying, in essence, I wish that you were kings that we could get alongside and rule with you. But, for now, you are not ready to be kings, because you are too worldly. Though Paul did not live like a king from the world's viewpoint, he viewed himself as a king, a king with the promise to be with God and reign for all eternity. Paul wanted the Corinthians' perception of themselves—and therefore their behavior— to line up with the reality of their spiritual identity.

What exactly does this fact—that believers are kings—mean for us today? Far from puffing up our pride, it should greatly humble us that we have such great standing and responsibility before the King of kings.

So what does a king look like? Let's look at some kingly traits that we should be striving to reflect:

- Kings have authority (rule, reign).
- Kings walk nobly, although humbly (at least, they should).
- Kings use justice and righteousness to establish their kingdoms.
- Kings need wisdom to govern the people.
- Kings fight battles to protect their homelands.
- Kings use counselors in their planning.

The King's actions affect the nation. As the king goes, so goes the nation. Let's take a closer look at some of these characteristics.

How Does a King Reign?

A king rules and reigns over his kingdom. The Word plainly says that the saints will reign over the nations (2 Timothy 2:12, Revelation 5:10, Revelation 20:6, Revelation 22:5). It also says that we shall judge the world and angels (1 Corinthians 6:2,3). Now that is authority. We will even have authority over Heavenly beings!

In her biography, one former witch shared how she could see a powerful and glorious authority when believers would walk by her. Unfortunately, she learned not to fear them because they did not realize the authority they had and therefore were no threat to her.

What a tragedy! As kings reigning in God's kingdom, we are to serve and protect the "lands" (homes, families, work environments, neighborhoods) God has given us. When believers are not wielding their spiritual authority, Satan has free reign. It is a bit like marauding invaders coming into the kingdom and plundering the king's lands and his people while the king sits oblivious on his throne. If only the king had used his royal authority to unleash the royal army to protect his people! Instead, the kingdom is plundered just outside his walls.

Believers have God-given authority to reign until He comes. In Matthew 28:18–20, nkjv Jesus said, "All authority has been given to Me in heaven and on earth." He then transferred this authority to us and commanded us to go and make disciples of all nations, baptizing and teaching them all things. His promise is to be with us always, even to the end of the age. Jesus would not have given us such a difficult task without also giving us the authority to achieve it.

In business, we know that it is foolish for a manager to try to accomplish something without the authority to do so. As kings, we are the managers of Jesus' kingdom. He gave us an assignment and the power to carry it out. That authority comes from His abiding presence in us, which will never leave us nor forsake us (Hebrews 13:5). We need to start believing it.

We have power. We have authority. We will rule and reign with Christ. When He appears, we will also appear with Him in glory (Colossians 3:4). Apply this truth to your prayer life. "Lord, I come as a king to your throne. I believe this prayer will rule this situation. I claim Proverbs 21:1, kjv for my life: "The king's heart is in the hand of the LORD, as the rivers of water: he turneth it whithersoever he will."

God uses our prayers to change nations, to set prisoners free, to change the course of human history. We have the authority and the mandate to do this. It is time, saints, that we start believing God. Let your prayers be kingly prayers of power. Wield your authority for His kingdom. Satan and all his demonic hosts will flee from the least saint who believes and acts on this truth.

How Does a King Walk?

What should your kingly walk look like? Well, kings walk nobly. They have a certain royal stride. Can you picture a king limping or crawling around on all fours? Nebuchadnezzar was one such king. One day, he had a stride that made nations tremble. The next day, the Lord humbled him because of his pride, and for the next seven years, he crawled around on the floor like a wild animal. After the allotted time, Nebuchadnezzar humbled himself, gave glory to God, and was restored back to his kingdom.

We were once like Nebuchadnezzar—living like wild animals, thinking that we were the kings of our own destiny, acting as we pleased, and foolishly believing that we accomplished things by our own power. But our time of humbling came and we confessed that Jesus is the King of Kings. With this confession, Jesus restored us back to His kingdom.

We now need to show forth a heavenly stride. Let your walk in life show forth the glory and praise of God. As they watch you, people should think, "Who is this person? They seem noble and powerful." We should lead others by our nobility, a walk that clearly shows to whom we belong.

How Does a King Act?

Proverbs clearly says that justice establishes the king's throne. Kings who do evil are misusing their authority. The king's sword was not put there by accident. God instituted it for justice. When we review the lives of the kings in Israel and Judah after the kingdom split, we see that only a handful did what was right in the eyes of the Lord. We also see the consequences. It was not pretty.

Judah maintained some just and righteous kings, and we can easily see the Lord's hand of blessing and strength on them. Eventually, a king was so just and righteous that his justice actually united the divided nation—King David.

Here was a man after God's own heart. His faith and trust in God became evident as he rose from shepherd boy to the throne. He guided Israel with skillful hands and became a shepherd of God's people.

As kings over the territory allotted to us, we need the same skillful hands to do our own shepherding of God's people. Our territory may be our own households, our neighborhoods, or our cities or states. Whatever geography God has given us, we should live justly and at peace with all men and should let the righteousness of Christ come out in our actions.

Jesus said, "Let your light shine before men, so that they may see your good deeds and praise your father in heaven" (Matthew 5:16). "Let your conscience be clear before men and God" (Acts 24:16). This is kingly behavior. Be quick to confess your sins and faults and be longsuffering with others.

This is a prerequisite for kingship, which is also a life of service. To be useful to God, we must have short accounts with God and man. Then God will trust us to a ministry that uses our gifts and talents for His glory. If he can trust us, then we have become His friends.

6

God's friends

Greater love hath no man than this, that a man lay down his life for his friends. Ye are my friends, if ye do whatsoever I command you. Henceforth I call you not servants, for the servant knoweth not what his Lord doeth: but I have called you friends; for all things that I have heard of my Father I have made known unto you. (John 15:13–15, kjv)

Jesus called His disciples "friends." Why? Because He decided to trust them. He decided to love them. He decided to commit to them and open up to them. A servant is available at a moment's call, but this relationship is more distant and obligatory. It wasn't the relationship that Jesus was looking for. He held back nothing from His followers and risked everything for them.

Jesus set a standard for us to follow. By this definition, the greatest expression of love and friendship is the willingness to lay down our lives for another. This is a primary theme of Jesus' earthly ministry and the apostolic teachings.

Jesus prophesied that, at the time of the end, the love of most would grow cold (Matthew 24:12). I think His prophecy has come true. Our supply of love is low, even though the demand for love is high. It is my opinion that the church also registers low on sacrifice.

We, in the United States, are the most independent, affluent society in the world, but our love is incomplete. Friends are in short supply. When life becomes difficult, it is not unusual to find that no one is really there for you.

If we are interested in being friends with the Master, there is a condition we must meet. We must obey His commands. People who simply live however they want to live are not friends of the Lord. To be His friends, we must follow His example of love and be willing to lay down our lives for Him. That is part of an obedient Christian life.

Since Jesus showed us what real love is like, we should follow in His footsteps. After all, if you cannot love the Lord, you cannot love anyone else. He is perfect in every way and is the most loving friend anyone can imagine. If we can't love Him, whom can we love? The reverse is also true. If we cannot love someone else, it reveals our lack of love toward God. We need to rely on His love to love others by allowing His love to flow through us. Our natural, human love runs out over time.

So, where is our relationship with the Lord? Since the love among believers is so low, our relationship with Jesus needs to be re-evaluated. The vertical relationship between God and man has a horizontal component. In 1 John 4:20, the Apostle John writes that you cannot say that you love God but hate your brother. These things are incompatible.

What can you do if you think that you are not God's friend the way you should be? This can change if you commit to Him, trust in Him, and seek to pursue this relationship with all your heart. It is amazing how quickly love can be poured out if you come honestly and sincerely before our God.

I, myself, have let the Lord down. Especially going back to my early college ministry days, I was particularly prone to falling into relationships that were not pleasing to Him. When I failed Him, He showed me that, whenever I sinned, it was like hammering nails into His hands and feet all over again.

There was a direct relationship between my sin and Jesus' torturous death on the cross. This revelation changed my life. From that time on, I committed to being His friend. For the first time, I had a hatred for sin. It was a gift to think and feel this way. It cannot be conjured up out of religious effort or show.

Can God Trust You?

The Lord needs to be able to trust us. If He calls to us and we do not respond, we show ourselves to be spiritually irresponsible. God desires to fully trust us. However, if we are not faithful, we limit what He reveals to our hearts. It is written, "Come close to me and I will come close to you…" (James 4:8). If we are not drawing close to God, He has no obligation to draw near to us or to share His truth with us.

There is another saying that may be familiar: "Do not cast your pearls before swine" (Matthew 7:6, kjv). God has reached out in tenderness and trust, and without realizing it, we often turn and tear Him to pieces. The Bible calls this "crucifying the Son of Man afresh" (Hebrews 6:6, kjv). Would you consider someone your friend if they crucified you? They may claim to be your friend all day long ("Many a man claims to have unfailing love, but a faithful man, who can find?" Proverbs 20:6), but their actions speak louder than words.

I used to think that everyone was my friend and that I loved everybody. I also thought that everyone felt the same way about me as I did about them. A bit naïve, you think?

Now, I realize that if you have two or three friends in your lifetime, you are doing great. Real friends are the kind who sticks closer than a brother; the kind who believe in you when everything goes wrong; the kind who, if they hear a stray word spoken about you will stick up for you; the kind who show up on your doorstep when trouble arrives.

Oh, how the Lord wants friends like that! Friends He can share with and they will treasure His Words (Isaiah 66:1,2), pray about them, act on them, and change their lives because of them.

It is part of every believer's spiritual heritage to be a friend of God. It is ours for the taking. But it is not easy to do. It carries with it responsibility, sacrifice, and above all, love.

A Worthy Sacrifice

In Spring 2005, I co-hosted a Christian radio program based in Little Rock, AK, called "Friends of God." It was a talk-based radio show focused on encouraging believers to seek the Lord in their daily lives and to learn how to overcome life's issues through the Word of God and prayer. It was a very fun program and yet very serious and challenging.

It was challenging because people in life struggle with so many issues and have so many needs. When we allow people to really open up to us, their needs can seem overwhelming.

Once the depth of the need becomes apparent, we may even want to run away. But years ago, the Lord taught me to embrace all believers and not turn away from any that He sends. Jesus Himself said, "Give to everyone who asks you..." (Luke 6:30). I have lived according to that revelation and it has born much fruit over the years.

Recently, a friend of mine (I'll call her Jane) was dealing with this very issue. She had noticed that a cashier at the grocery store looked frazzled and upset. She asked if everything was okay, and to her surprise, the woman began to pour her heart out to her.

After talking a few minutes, it became clear that the cashier was a Christian, but she was struggling with lack of peace and joy. Jane asked about her spiritual life, whether she was reading the Bible and having regular prayer time, and the woman said that she had not.

Jane encouraged her in these areas and promised to pray for her. For several months, Jane's path did not cross with the woman. Then, one day, she recognized the cashier as she was heading to the check-out line. But instead of stopping to see how she was doing, Jane deliberately chose another line.

Jane was struggling with her own personal and family issues, and she, herself was feeling depleted and in need of encouragement. While Jane was thankful that she had been given the opportunity to minister to the woman earlier, she didn't feel that she had the reserves to follow up with someone who clearly had such deep needs.

A month or so later, Jane saw the woman again. Just as the time before, Jane was still struggling emotionally and headed for another line. The Holy Spirit strongly convicted her this time, and she reminded herself, "Show love to the brethren, for they will know you by your love," and went back to the woman's line.

At first, as the cashier checked out her items, Jane hoped she wouldn't recognize her. Then, nudged by the Spirit, she engaged the woman and asked how she was doing. Jane reminded the woman of her earlier conversation, and the cashier suddenly beamed from ear to ear.

"Jane, right?" she asked. "I remember." She then told Jane that she was doing extremely well, that she had taken Jane's advice and had been reading her Bible and it had made a huge difference in her life. "There was a time when I was not reading," she admitted, then joked, "but then I said, 'But Jane told me to read it, and if I don't, she will be mad at me.' So I started again. Now I'm doing great!"

Jane felt a stab of conviction. Earlier, she had been so selfish about stopping, too self-absorbed to take the time to show care and concern for a fellow believer.

Now, not only was that believer not going to "take up too much of her time," as she had feared, but the woman's testimony was encouraging her! By being a friend to this woman, Jane has also been a friend to the Lord.

It's Not Your Choice

If we are living by the Spirit, we don't choose our friends. We embrace anyone whom God brings to us without partiality. Hopefully, these words will bring something fresh and new to your life. Pray and ask God to bring ones you can love and befriend. As far as it depends on you, be their friend, be their family.

In this way, you show yourself to belong to the one friend we can all count on, the Lord. The Lord desires to trust us—to really open up to us. He is looking for friends who are worthy of His call. He shed His blood, and by doing so, forever proved His friendship to us.

That sacrifice has made us into a new people, into individuals whose handiwork is of God. One could say we are now masterpieces of our God.

7

masterpieces

For we are God's masterpiece. He has created us anew in Christ Jesus, so we can do the good things He planned for us long ago. (Ephesians 2:10, nlt)

The Greek word here in Ephesians 2:10 for masterpiece is poiēma, which translates a "thing that is made." I have heard one person infer that the word "poem" comes from this Greek word, poiēma. It makes sense to me that we are a poem from God. Our lives are written by God unto His glory and for His sweet purposes.

A companion verse that uses the same Greek word is Romans 1:20 which says "For the invisible things of Him from the creation of the world are clearly seen, being understood by the things that are made (poiēma)."

The Bible teaches that we are God's creation, a thing He has made in His own image and likeness. We are His workmanship, His handiwork, and yes, His Masterpiece. We are the center of His creation, made in His image for His glory.

God has made us into individuals with unique talents, abilities, and personalities. No two people are exactly alike, not even identical twins, of which I am one.

Did you realize that you are a Masterpiece? Please close your eyes and consider this truth that the Bible teaches. You are a Masterpiece! (silent pause)

My spouse once said to me that I was a work of art. It was perhaps the best compliment I have ever received. But she is not the only one who feels this way about me. God feels this way about me too, and also about you.

We are a work of art, of beauty, of grace and love. Do not let anyone fool you, my dear friend; God does not make junk. He knew what He was doing when He made you. You are special. You are made for His purpose. You are the apple of His eye. Undoubtedly, many of you are saying, "Brother, you don't even know me. There is no way I am a Masterpiece anything."

Is that right? So God is lying and you are telling the truth? Listen, if God says it, then it is true. The real challenge is whether you will believe it and receive it into your life. No one can force you to believe anything.

My experience is that these truths in the Bible are for our transformation, our edification and our correction.

Now when God says you are His Masterpiece, a work of art, it is not His intent to hang you on a wall for others to admire you. No, He made you into the special person you are for a purpose, to be of service and help to others wherever He places you. Bloom where you are planted for His glory and by His grace you will make a difference.

There is another verse that says we are complete in Him (Colossians 2:10, kjv). It is not necessary to have another person for us to be complete as long as we are in God.

However, according to the Bible, there is nothing wrong with having someone else in your life in the commitment of marriage. Two can achieve more than one, their return is good (Ecclesiastes 4:9-12).

Many people feel empty and alone, but if you realize that you are a Masterpiece, complete in Him, it will fill your life with meaning, purpose, and hope.

Don't just read through these words and go on. If you sense the prompting of God, deeply consider and meditate on them. Make these verses your own and thank the Lord you are His Masterpiece, and freely share this new found truth.

Do the Good Things

According to Ephesians 2:10, you have been created anew in Christ to do good things, to do good works. You are not saved by good works but they come as a natural result of being saved and being re-created anew in the Savior. Does that make sense?

Many get this backward, thinking that if only they can do enough to please God, then maybe He will forgive them. But this is not the gospel. Jesus took care of satisfying His Father's justice by dying for our sins on the Cross, so we could be forgiven once and for all supernaturally. He took our sins upon himself and the righteous brought the unrighteous to God through this one-time sacrifice.

Once this is accepted and received (John 1:12) by any person in any culture or background, that person is born again and is given new life in Christ.

This new life is the very person of God living inside you (his name is the Holy Spirit) and doing His work in you to transform you into the image of His dear Son, and to help you carry out, by faith, all the good things God has planned for you before the foundation of the world.

This is mind-blowing, but God has predestined you to accomplish certain things while on planet earth before you go to your heavenly home. If you walk by faith and are sensitive to His leading and prompting in the Holy Spirit, you will begin the faith adventure to serve the Only Wise God and to do the good planned for you before you were born.

I am not encouraging you to be a good person and try your best to help people. That is not where I am going. God, who is good, will co-labor with you to carry out His will in all things, if you allow Him to.

Self View

This new found truth is how God really sees you, as a Masterpiece. Just about any counselor, social worker, or mental health clinician will share that it is all about how a person sees himself. There is significant truth in this vantage point. If you can believe and accept God's view, as He created you then your value and worth will rise dramatically in your own eyes.

How does this self-view affect anything? Do you think that the devil wants you to recognize how valuable and special you really are? Of course not. The truth we are focusing on is that you are made anew in Christ Jesus to live out your true identity as belonging to Him.

And if you belong to Him, then the things you do and say will reflect that good. God has these good things for you to do because you are His Masterpiece in a corrupt and fallen world. You will shine like lights in the world by just being yourself (Philippians 2:16).

Not only that, but Ephesians 2:10 says that God has planned these good things in advance for you to do them, to walk in them, and to live them out. We are meant to do good, much good during our time on the earth. Isn't that awesome? You can wake up this morning and proclaim, "Lord, I am here and available to perform all the good you have planned for me to do since you have created me for it."

The Bible has such sweet and kind words to say about you. Words that heal, words that soothe, words that make a difference in life and death. Take this Word for you and run with it. Embrace it and do not let anyone or anything sell you short of it.

In summary, you are God's Masterpiece- special, unique, and talented. Allow Him the full reign and control in your heart, and He will direct all your life toward the good He has planned. It is important to take God at His Word and to accept your beauty, your usefulness, and your intended purpose- to help others become all they can be in Him by learning and applying His truths in the Bible to their lives.

The result of a life that realizes and acts upon this truth will yield eternal dividends and leave behind a legacy that will span generations to come. No riches, possessions, or career field can compare to this return if we only believe and live according to that belief.

When we do believe, something fundamentally changes in and through us. We become new creatures in Him.

8

new creatures

Therefore, if any man be in Christ, he is a new creature, old things are passed away, behold all things are become new. (2 Corinthians 5:17, kjv)

When a person is born again or born from above, there is a fundamental shift in his spiritual identity. Although the born-again person may look basically the same on the outside, the inner man of the heart—who he truly is—has changed. He has been created after the new man in righteousness and true holiness (Ephesians 4:24).

This is a mystery, but the Bible says that a believer has become a child of God, not born naturally, but of the Spirit (John 1:12,13). The Book of Titus summarizes this miracle by saying, "Not by works of righteousness which we have done, but according to his mercy he saved us, by the washing of regeneration, and renewing of the Holy Ghost." (Titus 3:5,kjv).

A Basic "DNA" Change

At the moment of salvation, the spiritual "DNA" of a believer changes. This transformation, which Jesus called the new birth, both washes and renews us. The physical body has not changed, but the spirit of the person has been "born again" through regeneration.

Through the Spirit, Jesus Christ has come into the human heart to take up residence and, if allowed, take over every area to God's glory.

I have seen this "born-again" experience even make a person look better than before because the joy of salvation shines right out from the hidden man of the heart. It's like getting a haircut, manicure, steam bath, and workout all rolled up into one.

This is a divine operation. Once it occurs, the person has a new frequency on which they can function—a direct wireless connection to Heaven's throne. The password to gain access to this throne is simple to remember: Jesus! What a name!

So powerful is this name that Peter and John were commanded by the religious leaders of their day not to even speak it. But their response was that they could not help speaking about what they had seen and heard (Acts 4:20). Earlier, they had declared that there is no other name under heaven by which man must be saved (Acts 4:12).

The New Testament makes it clear that there was the first Adam and then there was the second Adam, Jesus. 1 Corinthians 15:22, kjv states, "For as in Adam all die, even so in Christ shall all be made alive." One man, Adam, was from the earth and perished, as did all who came after him.

But Jesus, the man from Heaven, brought eternal life that is now available to all who follow after Him. What a promise from God's Word! This is great news for all mankind.

From the time of the Fall, when Adam and Eve disobeyed God's "house rules," sin reigned and lead to death. But the second Adam, Jesus, died for our sins once for all and brought eternal life and salvation to all who believe.

Jesus is the Captain of our Salvation (Hebrews 2:10 kjv), the Author of Life (Acts 3:15), the Great I AM (John 18:6), the Prince of Peace (Isaiah 9:6), the Overcomer of the World (John 16:33), and Mighty God (Isaiah 9:6).

An individual who puts his or her faith in Jesus literally becomes a new creature. Everything has changed. Their world has been turned right side up. They begin to see things in the light of God and His Word, which is spirit and truth.

What Kind of Fruit Are You Bearing?

John the Baptist told the people of Israel that they should bear fruit in keeping with repentance, to have something to "show" in our new lives with Christ. Although good works do not earn salvation for anyone, it is clear that God has called us to do good works to fulfill His calling on, and design for, us as new believers (Ephesians 2:10). In fact, Jesus has laid upon all believers a grave responsibility. He said that by our fruit the world will recognize us as Christians.

What a responsibility we carry to bear fruit worthy of His name! Our conversion is one of moving from darkness to light. We used to do wrong naturally and instinctively, but now it is natural to do what is right.

God lives in unapproachable light, and we are His offspring. His Spirit can and will graciously guide us into all truth for every situation.

We were once friends with the world and thought as the world thinks. Now, we are aliens and strangers in the world (1 Peter 2:11), children of God in a crooked and depraved generation, where we are to shine like stars (Philippians 2:15).

Going from being an unbeliever to being a believer is a scary transition and it is one that most are not prepared for. Until you've done it, you cannot imagine what it is like. It is like waking up and seeing reality for the first time.

In the movie, *The Matrix*, Neo learned that nothing in his world was as it seemed. In fact, the world he knew was a computer-generated program. Everything he believed to be reality was false, part of the programming.

Instead of humans controlling the world, machines were harvesting humans as living batteries to energize their own existence. Different rules and principles applied, depending on which reality you were living in at the time.

This is a rough illustration of the transformation in our worldview that occurs when we become believers. Unlike *The Matrix*, where reality was darker and more sinister than it seemed, reality under Jesus is brighter and more wonderful than we can imagine. However, it is still very different, often upside-down from what we had thought before.

All Things Become New

The Bible emphatically states that when we become believers, we become new creatures. We can clearly see reality the way it really is. We can see things from God's perspective, which is based on truth and love, not from our own subjective and limited viewpoints.

Best of all, we no longer are resigned to the fate of always falling short—missing the mark—of God's plan for our lives. Empowered by the Holy Spirit, we have the potential to grow into the people God created us to be.

Each individual is meant to be conformed to the image of God's Son, Jesus, and His goal is for us to be like Him in every way. This is not meant to be a religious exercise, for believers to carry around a long list of do's and don'ts to live by.

Rather, I'm talking about a radical transformation of the heart that allows believers to conform to the inner life of the Spirit that Jesus taught by His own example. I pray that you seek the Lord about what it means to truly be a new creature in Christ.

Commit yourself to being that person God has created you to be. Open yourself to His light through the Word, prayer, and biblical fellowship with other believers.

Square Peg in a Round Hole

Are there any downsides to being a new creature in Christ? It all depends on your viewpoint. Do you consider your own goals and desires to be more important than God's? Once you allow the Holy Spirit to transform you, you will not fit into the world's mold anymore.

Your spiritual being will be alive and central in your life, and you will view things from an eternal perspective, not just what seems fun, interesting, or exciting at the time. You will not only be living for today but for eternity, for what is helpful to others and especially to the Kingdom of God.

In Matthew 6:25–33, Jesus promised that if we "seek first" His kingdom and His righteousness, "all these things" (clothes, food, and other necessities) will be added to us.

Think about all the time we spend worrying about how we are going to pay our bills, fix the car, or deal with those problems with the kids. Once we shift our focus from the daily grind—those things that bog us down and distract us from our trusting relationship with Christ—and focus on the Kingdom of God, God will take care of the rest.

It doesn't mean that we stop fulfilling our responsibilities. Rather, it simply means that our first concern is pleasing God. When it is, the problems of life naturally prioritize themselves. As long as we are doing what God calls us to do, we can trust that He is working out everything else for our good (Romans 8:28).

God will always give good gifts to His children, even if it does not seem that way at the time. He has a plan to prosper you, not to harm you. You are no longer a child of wrath. You have become His adopted son or daughter (John 1:12, Gal. 3:26, 1 John 3:10, Rom. 9:8), and He has some serious affection and attention that He wants to lavish on you.

This doesn't mean that He always works out the details of our lives the way we expect Him to (He doesn't), or even that the way He works things out is always comfortable to us (it isn't).

As a child of God, He promises that, regardless of our outward circumstances, He is using everything for our good. He knows and controls the bigger picture. This takes a huge burden off your shoulders, doesn't it? Just do what God asks of you, then leave the rest to Him. Whew! What a relief.

So there is a tradeoff. Being a child of God involves taking responsibility and being committed to walking the path God has set forth and revealed through His Spirit.

By being committed and taking responsibility, we have His promise that everything will be okay in the end, even though it might not seem like it at the time.

God loves you and desires for you to realize just how precious you are to Him. No matter your past, you are new in Him, your future is fresh and bright, and He desires for you to realize that you are new in the spirit. You have become new spiritual beings.

9

spiritual beings – part one

Yet a time is coming and has now come when the true worshipers will worship the Father in the Spirit and in truth, for they are the kind of worshipers the Father seeks. God is spirit, and His worshipers must worship in the Spirit and in truth. (John 4:23-24)

In the above John 4 passage, Jesus is speaking to the Samaritan woman at the well and says a profound thing to her, revealing a truth concerning the nature of God.

God Is Spirit

Sometimes the simplest truths are the most profound. God is spirit. We are made in God's image, but we appear to be human beings, made of flesh and bone. The Bible is clear that our body is natural and wasting away and that the real us is invisible inside our bodies-that is our spirit. That is the real us.

The Bible says that outwardly we are wasting away, yet inwardly we are being renewed day by day (2 Corinthians 4:16). What a contrast. One – our body - is decreasing in function and usefulness while the other – our spirit - is just getting started and is growing. So, which one should we invest the most heavily in?

I am an advocate of taking care of our body since we are stewards of it and we can live longer and more productive lives if we take good care of it. If we eat nutritionally, exercise consistently, rest well, and maintain balance, we will extend our usefulness. But, I believe we should invest more heavily in our spiritual life.

The reasons are obvious. That is who we really are. The body we have for at most 100 years, but the spirit is eternal. The spirit is the heart and core of our lives. If we properly maintain our spirit, the rest falls into place.

Our spirit (and its maintenance) should be the highest priority of our lives. But, evidence indicates that the human race has been unaware of this truth that Jesus shares with the Samaritan woman. God is spirit and so are we.

Food and Drink for the Spirit

Just as the body needs nourishment (food and drink) for energy and optimal function, in the same way, so does the spirit. But what does one feed the spirit? As you might expect, the Bible has some answers:

> *The Spirit gives life; the flesh counts for nothing. The words I have spoken to you – they are full of the Spirit and life. (John 6:63)*

> *When your words came, I ate them; they were my joy and my heart's delight, for I bear your name, Lord God Almighty. (Jeremiah 15:16)*

So, we see from these verses that the spirit in us has to eat to maintain health, just like our bodies. Our spirit must have communion and fellowship with Jesus and other believers or we will be hungry in our spirit.

When you stop eating and drinking, you will become sluggish, out of energy and unable to perform normal functions. It is the same way when our spirit does not plug into Jesus and His Body. One effective way to do that is to receive His words in the Bible consistently.

Born Again

In John 3, Nicodemus approached Jesus at night and Jesus confided in Israel's teacher that he must be born again. Thinking in a worldly way, Nicodemus asked how he could enter his mother's womb to be born a second time. He was thinking physically, not spiritually. Jesus knew the real birth that has eternal implications is the spiritual birth. Nicodemus already experienced the first birth, but to be alive spiritually, he needed a second birth. This is a spiritual birth. Every true believer in Jesus is born again spiritually and has a spiritual birth into this new life.

Keep Feasting

Hopefully, you have entered into this spiritual birth. Does a baby stop eating after they have been born? No, they are just beginning, right? You need God's milk initially, and then other food as you mature spiritually into the person God has meant for you to be. Some beginning steps to get God's milk (like a mother's breast) deals with using the Bible as the main feeding source.

Getting His Word into Our Spirit

There are four main ways to get God's Word into our spirits. One can read it, hear it, memorize it, and study it. Then we must digest this word through our spirit so that it provides nutrients to our soul and works its way out into our practical daily lives.

The best way to do this is to meditate on His word, mulling and considering what you have taken in by allowing your spirit to further break it down into its elemental truths.

Joshua reinforces this principle of meditating on God's Word to experience success in your life:

> *Do not let this book of the law depart from your mouth, meditate on it day and night, so that you may be careful to do everything written in it. Then you will be prosperous and successful. (Joshua 1:8)*

God's Spirit Makes His Home with You

Jesus promises that when we have faith in Him, that He sends another counselor to be with us forever- the Spirit of Truth (John 14:16-17). This Holy Spirit comes into us by faith and takes up His residence inside our hearts, making Himself united with our spiritual being.

In other words, there is now no way to separate your inner spiritual being from God's Holy Spirit, who seals and keeps you for the day of redemption (Ephesians 1:13-14).

All Spirits Are Alive To God

God does not view things in the same way we view them. He has an eternal perspective and it would be helpful if we would adjust our perspective accordingly.

Speaking of the patriarchs Jesus says,

> *"But in the account of the burning bush, even Moses showed that the dead rise, for he calls the Lord 'the God of Abraham, and the God of Isaac, and the God of Jacob.' He is not the God of the dead, but of the living, for to Him all are alive." (Luke 20:37-38)*

So all are alive to God. Each person has a spirit. God desires each person to live in the spirit and to live for Him so that His Holy Spirit can guide and help them. Unfortunately, not every person is willing to make this decision. God does not force or coerce anyone into His Kingdom to worship Him and to live for truth.

Hearing and Receiving

As I have matured and seen the significance of the spiritual aspect and its preeminence for life, I want to leave you with two practices that have helped me to continue my growth (and I am still far from arriving).

The first is to hear God's voice in all of life - nature, music, others, words, films, silence, etc. God speaks life and peace and grace to all who humble themselves.

Second, open yourself to receive from God all he has for you, especially love, peace, mercy, and grace. Receive into your spirit these attributes of God to represent Him adequately in a fallen world.

The Lord will bless you as you do.

10

spiritual beings - part two

The Spirit gives life; the flesh counts for nothing. (John 6:63)

One of the most important aspects of our spiritual identity, as we discussed in the last chapter, is that we are spiritual beings.

Not only is God spirit, but we are spirit, too. For a very short time, we are encased in these bodies of flesh, but as the Apostle Paul put it, this earthly tent (our bodies) will be folded up one day.

When that happens, the "real us" will still be around. Now we know that if the earthly tent we live in is destroyed, we have a building from God, an eternal house in heaven, not built by human hands. (2 Corinthians 5:1)

As a spiritual being, your identity is not in the things of this world. One day, you'll leave them all behind. This is why it's so important, right now, that we lay down anything that would prevent us from pursuing God's plan for us. That means letting go of anything not guided and directed by the Holy Spirit. In other words, letting go of everything in the flesh.

Easier Said Than Done

Of course, this is easier said than done. Many believers wonder why, if they are now spiritual beings, they have such great struggles and still act like the same people they used to be. Little seems to have changed for them. The reason is that, although we are spiritual beings, we have to choose to act like spiritual beings. The spiritual life is an abundant life, but it is a choice that has to be made. Then you have to walk in that choice, day in and day out.

Of course, Satan doesn't want you to live like the spiritual being—the child of God—that you really are. Satan will throw everything he has at you to try to dissuade you.

Your flesh doesn't want to live by the spirit, either. Instinctively, our flesh rebels against God's authority. Just like an unruly two-year-old rebelling against his parents, we decide to make the rules and do things our own way.

Although the flesh is not who we truly are, we are tempted to go back to our old ways, the way we used to live before we received the Lord. Consequently, we have two main forces vying for our true person: the flesh and the Spirit.

The Spiritual Boxing Ring

So what exactly is the flesh? The "flesh" can be described as your natural instincts before you accepted

Jesus into your life. It is the thoughts and actions that come from the heart and mind of the unsaved person. Even though some of these instincts can appear to be good, they are not born of Christ. Thus, they can never please God.

The Greek word for flesh is "sarx." In a general sense, sarx means our physical bodies to which sin can attach. Another Greek word, "soma", is also related to the physical body, but without the spiritual implications.

For use in this book, the word "flesh" does not refer to the physical body, soma, but to sarx, the part of our flesh that desires to be independent of God. It represents the self-life and all the survival tactics we use to live life on our own terms.

The flesh wants to protect itself. It wants to always defend its actions. (Do you feel that you always have to "win" an argument or a game? That's the flesh.) It wants to take the most convenient, expedient path. It does not want to esteem anyone or anything as more important than itself.

It can never show agape love, or God's immeasurable, unconditional love. Although fleshly sacrifice is possible, we know from Paul's description of love in 1 Corinthians 13 that, without God's love mixed in, it accomplishes nothing.

The acts of the Spirit, on the other hand, are born from Christ. They come from the new nature that God gives us after we accept the lordship of Jesus and put ourselves under His control. Only that which is done in the Spirit can please God.

The flesh and the Spirit war against one another. Therefore, part of embracing our true spiritual identity is learning to distinguish between the two. Once we can identify when the flesh raises its ugly head, like the popular child's game "Whack-A-Mole," we can bash it back down again.

Notice that we have the flesh both before and after salvation. The difference is that, after salvation, we do not need to submit to the flesh's control—its desires, impulses, ambitions, lusts, and the like. (See Galatians 5:19–21, especially kjv.) The Spirit of God indwells us after salvation to give us power against these impulses.

Even with this power, it is still a daily battle. Paul said that even he had to crucify his flesh (or "nail" his fleshly desires to the cross) on a daily basis (1 Corinthians 15:31). Believe me. I know how hard this is.

My flesh still regularly raises its ugly head, although less and less as I grow in Christ. The Lord seems to just shift to new areas of the flesh that need work. One day, you might struggle with lust. Another day, you might struggle with prideful ambition. Yet another day, you might struggle with control issues.

The Lord is faithful to help us overcome each of these desires, in turn, if our commitment and spiritual disposition are to press hard after Him.

How do you recognize when the flesh or the Spirit is operating? A listing of the distinctive fruits of each can be seen in Galatians 5:16–26, a list that I think is particularly helpful in kjv. Please take a minute to read this passage.

The flesh and the spirit are contrary to one another. In Galatians 5, scripture says that the flesh manifests itself as adultery, fornication (sex outside of marriage), uncleanness (inward or outward things that defile a person), idolatry (worship of images other than God), witchcraft, hatred, strife (conflict through disharmony with others), heresies (rejection of the established Word), envy, murder, drunkenness, and so on.

Those who do these things will not inherit the Kingdom of God. By contrast, the fruit of the Spirit is love, joy, peace, longsuffering (patience despite annoyance over a long period of time), gentleness, goodness, faith, meekness (submissive humbleness), and temperance (avoiding excesses).

Of course, while the scriptures only mention the "big" sins by name, the flesh can manifest itself in many ways— little things that may seem unimportant to you but that are still important to God. For example, when you let loose your tongue to criticize or judge. When you take that last piece of cake, even though you know that someone else wants it.

When you angrily honk at that slow driver in front of you. Yes, these are "the little things," but it is in these things that God judges our faithfulness and seriousness about following His commands. Jesus warned that, if a man cannot be trusted with little, he cannot be trusted with much (Luke 16:10).

If we look at it this way, the "little things" are not so little at all. They are big things because they are the stick by which God measures us. In the Song of Solomon, these things are described as the little foxes that ruin the vines, stripping the bark, causing the whole plant to wither and die, never producing the fruit of which it was capable of (Song of Solomon 2:15).

So this is the flesh. Not a pretty picture is it? Praise God that we no longer have to be influenced, controlled, and mastered by it!

Identifying the Flesh

So how can we identify when the flesh starts to raise its ugly head? There are several steps you can take to recognize the flesh and whack this ugly "mole" back into its place.

First, recognize that you are a spiritual being. When the U.S. Treasury officers are trained to combat counterfeiting, they are first trained to identify what the original U.S. currency looks like. If you don't know the truth, how can you identify the fake? The same goes for your spirit. Before you can recognize the flesh, you have to first recognize the spirit.

For those of you old enough to remember, there used to be a game show on television in which the contestants would be told that one in three people was of a certain sort: an astronaut, a juggler, a physician. The contestants would then question all three to figure out which was the true person.

In the end, the host would say, "Will the real [whatever the person's name was], please stand up?" The panel of three contestants would then go through a series of fake standing gestures to keep the audience guessing who the real person was until the very end.

That's television. In reality, we never have to guess as to our real identity. No matter how much the flesh may look or feel like the real you, it isn't. Once the blood of Jesus saves you, your identity is in Christ. Period.

It isn't something you strive for. It is something you are. It's not just in your new position as a Christian, but in actual reality—an undeniable fact.

Second, once you know your true identity, you can start acting like it. A physician doesn't head to an attorney's office in the morning. He heads to a medical building.

A pro golfer doesn't clock in behind the hotel desk of the Marriott. He heads for the golf course. Likewise, once you know that your identity is in Christ, you start behaving accordingly.

This starts with reading His Word. If you don't have God's Word inside you, how will you know what He expects of you? You should make Bible reading and prayer an essential and vital part of your daily routine.

Next, ask God to show you when you are acting in the flesh. My own prayer has been, "Lord, if I do something that offends You, come down on me like a ton of bricks!"

That's another prayer He loves to answer! But don't stop at "show me." Ask Him to show you why you do those things. What makes someone want to gossip behind someone else's back? What makes a man want to put down his wife? What makes an employee want to argue with his boss?

God wants to reveal the reasons you do these fleshly things. Often, they are rooted in your past patterns and experiences. Once you know why you do them, you can more easily recognize and put a stop to them through His healing power and grace. His grace keeps us on course in our commitment to His Word and following His Spirit.

I want to give you an example from my own life. Sometime back, I was working at a company where the owner's daughter was very domineering and abusive. At this time, she was provoking a co-worker, who was brought to the verge of a nervous breakdown by her behavior.

My temper was rising against her, and one day, as it reached the boiling point, I openly shared with the Lord, "If she comes in here and abuses him one more time, I will bodily throw her out of the office!"

In response, the Lord showed me the passage where it says that it was to a man's glory to overlook an offense (Proverbs 19:11). What an awesome principle! I suddenly realized that every time I overlooked her mistreatment of my office mate, I gained glory in my life and heart. (While scripture is also clear that we should never turn our eyes or hearts away from mistreatment, bodily throwing her out of the office certainly wasn't the way to handle it!)

What a treasure I gained during those months. My office mate eventually quit, but I was transformed by God's grace. Except through prayer, the Lord did not allow me to deal directly with the boss's daughter concerning her wrong behavior at the time.

Though I was a comfort to my office worker, he was only so open to the Lord, limiting the impact I could have on him. I found out later that the boss's daughter was positively affected by these events, worked through them, and returned back to the Lord.

Walk, Live, Be Quench-Free

It is the Holy Spirit who enables us to do these things— things that would be impossible in our own strength. It is the Spirit who gives life. We are commanded repeatedly to walk in the Spirit, to live in the Spirit, not to quench the Spirit, and to take heed to the Spirit.

The Spirit quickeneth (John 6:63, kjv). He gives life where none is possible. The ultimate example is the resurrection of Christ. The same Spirit who raised Jesus from the dead now dwells in us by faith. What an unseen and yet unspeakable power the Holy Spirit is!

The Bible calls Him the Spirit of Jesus. He can place us in the triune (three-in-one) God in that state of oneness the world knows nothing about. The Spirit is that power that keeps us from engaging in the flesh. When we do not know how to pray, the Spirit helps us in our weakness.

The Spirit always overcomes the flesh. The Apostle Paul wrote:

> *For we know that our old self was crucified with him so that the body of sin might be done away with, that we should no longer be slaves to sin – because anyone who has died has been freed from sin. Now if we died with Christ, we believe that we will also live with him. For we know that since Christ was raised from the dead, he cannot die again; death no longer has mastery over him. The death he died, he died to sin once for all; but the life he lives, he lives to God. In the same way, count yourselves dead to sin but alive to God in Christ Jesus. (Romans 6:6–11)*

It is the Holy Spirit who gives us power over sin. While we might think our sin is too strong for even the Holy Spirit to overcome, or that God will turn His back and reject us if our sin is too great, the scriptures tell us that where sin is allowed to increase, God's grace increases all the more (Romans 5:20).

This may seem strange but think of sin as a weight. The more something weighs, the more strength is required to lift it. So the greater the temptation to sin, the more grace is necessary to "lift" it—the more His grace abounds.

This is an amazing biblical truth. No matter how hard you try to multiply the flesh, the Spirit is exponentially greater. By His power, your spirit can overpower the temptations of the flesh.

The Face in the Mirror

Do you know how all this is possible? By the One who lives inside of you. What does He look like? Although I have "majored" in the Spirit since I was a young Christian, I have learned that the Spirit is a lot more than I thought.

If you could take Him out of you and see what He looks like, do you have any idea what shape He would take? I will tell you a secret. It is a five-letter name beginning with J. That's right—Jesus! That is who the Spirit is. You cannot separate the Spirit and the person of Christ.

Although the Spirit and Christ are two separate persons, the Spirit is just as much God and carries out the role of communicating the desires of the Father and the Son. It is difficult to visualize the Spirit, especially in yourself.

But He is there nonetheless, desiring to help you in all aspects of life. When Jesus says that He will make His home in your heart, do you really think that He was speaking figuratively?

No! Through the Spirit, Jesus Himself lives in you. Yes, He is actually living inside you. What a miracle! It is almost too wonderful to consider. Christ in you is the hope of glory.

This anointing of God's Spirit in the believer is God's channel and path for our transformation and change. No wonder we will never be the same again!

In my walk with the Lord, I have learned that believers' understanding of their identity in Christ will make all the difference in how they grow and bear fruit.

You could say that the fundamental identity of the believer is an essential building block in spiritual growth. Why? Because all these verses in God's Word are given to strengthen and encourage us to live for God with all our potential.

If we do not believe and apply these truths, we go backward instead of forward in our goal to make progress in our faith. When you accept Jesus Christ as Lord, you become a new creature. The old things have passed away (2 Corinthians 5:17).

Do not allow Satan to sow a lie in your heart that you have no power over sin or no ability to please God. That is contrary to scripture.

The Word is clear that there is a battle raging, so know your position in Christ and don't budge from it. Don't give Satan a toehold by saying that you want to crucify the flesh (the niv sometimes translates this as the "sinful nature"[2]).

This just opens the door to excuse your failure. Reckon yourself already dead to sin (Romans 6:11). Your old man, who had a tendency and nature that was sinful, was crucified with Christ so that the body of sin might be destroyed.

From here on out, we must not serve sin.

> *Just as you used to offer the parts of your body in slavery to impurity and to ever-increasing wickedness, so now offer them in slavery to righteousness leading to holiness. (Romans 6:19)*

Wow! What a difference! Before Christ, our disposition was to yield our bodies to all kinds of sinful behaviors. Now, the command is to yield our bodies to what is right. We know that God gives the grace to make this possible.

Grace as an acronym has been said to mean "God's Riches at Christ's Expense." This grace is based on God's ability, not ours. Let God's grace flow freely in, through, and out of you to help others in their need.

Is There Religious Flesh?

Living in the spirit is not about looking good and acting well. It's not about behavior modification. Any attempt, in one's own strength, to live rightly and to do justly is nothing but "religious flesh." No one can live the Christian life without God's help. John 15 is all about the branches (believers) abiding in the vine (Jesus) so that we can bear fruit that blossoms from Him. It's a very simple principle.

No abiding, no fruit.

God expects you to be yourself—the self He designed for you, not some religious zealot trying to work out how you think you should be. That is why in Philippians 2:12, Paul writes, "... work out your salvation with fear and trembling." The work is not outward, but inward. It is a work of the Spirit. It is a gift of God's grace.

> *And God is able to make all grace abound to you, so that in all things at all times, having all that you need, you will abound in every good work. (2 Corinthians 9:8)*

What a verse! Get this one into your spirit. Apply it to your prayer life. God is able to complete the work He started in you until the day of the Lord's return (Philippians 1:6). But in order for this to occur, you must believe that He is able.

When you do, God freely offers His abundant grace. As you go about your day, you will have tests between the flesh and the spirit. When the roll call is made, make sure that only the spirit stands up. Do not give your flesh a place.

When you learn, with God's help, to know when your flesh is tempted to be activated, remind yourself strongly— speak the words out loud—about the Spirit knowing and helping you in time of need. The Spirit is able, but you must rely on Him and His promptings.

The inner man of the spirit can discern the issues of life and deal forthrightly with them. Will you trust the real you, the spirit man, to stand up when called?

How Does the Spirit See?

Once you put the Holy Spirit in His rightful place in your life, something wonderful happens. You will see not only yourself through the Spirit's eyes, but you will see others that way, as well. The Spirit does not see believers and unbelievers the same way.

The Spirit indwells believers and seals them, acting as a deposit, guaranteeing their salvation (Ephesians 1:13,14). It's like having a lifetime automatic deposit into your bank account.

Since riches are flowing into your account, you have resources in God to minister to the needs of others according to the riches He gives you in glory.

11

ministers

Not that we are sufficient of ourselves to think anything as of ourselves; but our sufficiency is of God; Who also hath made us able ministers of the New Testament; not of the letter, but of the spirit: for the letter killeth, but the spirit giveth life. (2 Corinthians 3:5–6, kjv)

The Bible says that we are made "able ministers" of the New Testament—not of the letter, but of the spirit. You might protest, saying, "Paul does not even know me. How can he say that I am made an able minister? I am no minister at all." Oh, how we think according to the world and the culture around us. Is the Bible meant to confuse us, tease us, or to put us down? Certainly not!

This is another great example of how we misunderstand our spiritual identity. We are able ministers because the scripture says that we are able ministers. And yet, something in us screams to avoid identifying with such a statement.

We are afraid that we will not be good ministers because we are taught that ministers run churches and administrate baptisms, communion, marriages, and funerals. Our fear keeps us from being the ministers God wants us to be.

We need to grow up in our faith and embrace what the Word reveals to us as truth. We can proclaim to the Lord, "I am an able minister of the New Testament by the Spirit. Whatever that means, Lord, it is for me. I embrace it. I receive it. I believe it. Now, let me love according to that foundational truth in my life. Let it be the core of my identity in Christ."

So what does an able minister do? An able minister strives to see needs and meet them. An able minister first and foremost focuses on serving others. Like David running to meet Goliath, he sees trouble and runs toward it.

An able minister does not flee but stands his ground. You may think, "I am just one person. What can I do?" But when the Philistines engaged the Israelites in the field of barley in Pas Dammim, all of Israel turned and fled from before them. But one Israelite warrior stood his ground and routed the entire Philistine army single-handedly. His arm was temporarily frozen on his sword and he could not let go of his grip. That is fighting hard, saints! Israel's army came back, but only for the spoil (2 Samuel 23:10).

I see this man as Christ in the New Testament. He takes his stand and no one can rout him—no one and nothing. This is the stand that we need to take.

You Are a Minister

An able minister stays close to the bosom of Christ and perseveres to obtain the victory over all the schemes of the devil. He trusts in the Lord at all times. Believe me, this is not easy. It requires a crucified life, a life of submission to the Father. We must learn to give up our own way and follow hard after the Master.

The fight for victory is a test of perseverance. Job experienced it and was an overcomer. He trusted the Lord and listened to His instruction. We know the result. God blessed him, and he ended up with twice as much as before.

This lines up with what is written in Zechariah 9:12-

> *"Return to your fortress, O prisoners of hope; even now I announce that I will restore twice as much to you."*

A prisoner does not have many rights but belongs completely to the keeper of the prison. Hopefully, you are a prisoner of the Lord. His yoke is easy and His burden is light (Matthew 11:30).

I can assure you, the devil does not function this way. Obviously, the word "minister" in 2 Corinthians 3 does not mean one's position as a leader of a congregation or a member of the clergy. It is merely the functional role of every believer in Jesus to perform his ministry according to the Spirit.

Every believer is a minister and every believer has a ministry, according to the Word. Earlier, when my friend Jane took the time to stop and show compassion for the cashier at the grocery store, she was being an able minister. Any time we offer to help, pray for someone who is hurting, contribute to a food drive— even donate blood— we are being able ministers.

Although there are lots of ways to minister, there is only one ministry in the New Testament—the ministry of the Spirit. Does that surprise you? It's true.

There is only one ministry. It's just that, whether, through faith, wisdom, prophecy, or another gift, it manifests itself in a variety of ways. "There are diversities of gifts, but the same Spirit. There are differences of ministries, but the same Lord. There are diversities of activities, but it is the same God who works all in all" (1 Corinthians 12:4-6, nkjv).

In other words, all of these individual ministries have the same purpose—to glorify God through the Body and to make His manifold wisdom known to the heavenly realms (Ephesians 3:10). There is a direct correlation between our ministry to the Lord and our ministry to others.

What this means is that we can only give others what we, ourselves, have received from above. If we aren't open to receiving the tools God desires to give us, then we will fail in the mission with which He has entrusted us.

This task is not beyond our reach. Jesus has already done the hard work. Now, all we need to do is rest in it. It is good for ministers of Christ to learn to enter Christ's rest.

It means that we cease from our own efforts and rely on God's mercy and grace (Romans 9:16, 2 Corinthians 12: 9,10). Resting doesn't mean that we cease from laboring (Hebrews 4:9–11). On the contrary, it is only when we cease from our own efforts that we become truly effective. Instead of relying on our own strength, which is limited, we rely on God's strength, which is unlimited.

This is why Paul wrote, "And He said to me, 'My grace is sufficient for you, for My strength is made perfect in weakness.' Therefore most gladly I will rather boast in my infirmities, that the power of Christ may rest upon me" (2 Corinthians 12:9, nkjv).

It's Not All About You

As a young believer trying to make a difference for the Lord's Kingdom, one thing I learned the hard way was that everything did not depend on me. This was a hard lesson because I wanted to control circumstances and people for the best possible outcome. Now I realize that God is sovereign and He does things a bit differently than I do.

God is much more concerned about our constitution, our character, and our inner life than our deeds. God desires to constitute us the right way, according to His dear Son. Once He does, He has no problem getting us to do the works He requires of us. The impact is there to boot, and it is much greater than we could ever accomplish on our own.

The main work of God is to believe and to rest in His finished work on the cross. This is sometimes easier said than done. We must learn to be responders to the Holy Spirit, not initiators. In other words, we listen to

His instruction, not try to tell Him what to do. This was tough for me. I am highly proactive, so before God could use me, He had to burn out of me my own ambition, desires, and life plans.

This took me much pain, turmoil, and struggle, but the end of it has been incredible. God is an expert at weaving these things together in His training program to accomplish His will and His way in our lives.

Some years back, I was the director of marketing for a division of a medium-sized engineering firm in Dayton, Ohio. I knew in my heart that God was leading me out of that job and into my own business, but I had a wife and children at home, so my desire for financial security prevented me from doing what God was leading me to do.

Still, I continued to pray and ask the Lord to show me His will. Every time, He pointed away from my current employer. Each time, I would respond by saying, "No, Lord, look toward my current employer, not away..." But He did not listen to me. It became clear that the Lord's will was to venture into self-employment, or as I like to call it. "God employment." Four months later, I was laid off from my job and started my own consulting firm.

I now realize that God wanted to stretch me, to help me to overcome my fears and my reliance on what I could see, hear, and touch and cause my faith and trust in Him to grow.

What does this have to do with being an able minister? When you own your own business, you become aware of your own lack of control and you learn to rely on God in ways you never had before. You have to learn to trust Him.

You also find yourself in the position of being responsible for other people and their families, as well as your own. This means defining your employees' work hours, responsibilities, and benefits. When it comes to payday, they get paid before you do. It's a highly effective environment in which for God to train you to become an able minister in all other areas of your life.

Building Blocks

One aspect of spiritual identity complements and builds on another. Each element is woven together like a tapestry that looks much more glorious than the individual threads.

This word "minister" is a great complement to the words "priest" and "saint." As an able minister, you are God's pinch hitter, His "go to guy" for whatever He wants you to do, whenever He wants you to do it, and for whomever He has in mind.

One day, you could be praying with someone. The next day, you could be sharing the gospel, preparing a meal, or laying hands on the sick. You should be prepared to take on those tasks, whatever they may be.

This is where the "rest in Christ's finished work" and "strength made perfect in weakness" become such an encouragement and motivator. He has not only given us the tasks, but the strength, power, and wisdom to accomplish them.

Certainly, we could never accomplish all of our responsibilities in our own strength. But when we enter His rest, it is His strength operating, not our own.

Even the priests in the Old Testament learned to rely on God's power to serve in the temple.

12

priests

From Jesus Christ, the faithful witness, the firstborn from the dead, and the ruler over the kings of the earth. To Him who loved us and washed us from our sins in His own blood, and has made us kings and priests to His God and Father, to Him be glory and dominion forever and ever. Amen.

And they sang a new song, saying: "You are worthy to take the scroll, And to open its seals; For you were slain, And have redeemed us to God by Your blood out of every tribe and tongue and people and nation, And have made us kings and priests to our God." (Revelation. 1:5–6, 5:9,10, nkjv)

What an interesting thought! We are priests in Christ to our God. It is clear from these passages that we are made priests by Jesus' sacrificial act, the shedding of His blood on the cross. It is not as if Jesus forced us to be priests.

We just simply are priests because of what He did. You also, as living stones, are being built up a spiritual house, a holy priesthood, to offer up spiritual sacrifices acceptable to God through Jesus Christ. (1 Peter 2:5, nkjv)

But you are a chosen generation, a royal priesthood, a holy nation. (1 Peter 2:9, nkjv) What exactly do priests do? Let's run through a biblical short list to shed more light on your identity as a priest.

Priests Offer Sacrifices to God

The first thing we notice about priests is that they offer regular sacrifices to God. In the Old Testament economy, priests were required to offer four kinds of sacrifices to continually cleanse and purify the people and the Holy Place inside the temple in Jerusalem:

Burnt offering

This was the blood sacrifice of an animal, such as a bull or goat sprinkled on the altar. The death of the animal represented the person offering the sacrifice and served as the person's substitute.

Grain offering

This was a "goodwill offering" to God consisting of flour, grain, or cakes, along with oil.

Fat offering

This offering was similar to the burnt offering except that the fat of the animal was offered. The meat was shared by the priests and the family of the one bringing the offering in celebration of their friendship with God.

Sin offering

When someone sinned against another person or God, the temple was defiled and had to be cleansed. The blood of an animal was sprinkled to symbolize that the sin had been forgiven.

Some of these sacrifices had to be offered daily. Others had to be offered weekly or monthly. Others were offered only on special occasions. With sacrifices being offered for individuals, as well as the nation, this required an entire system of Levitical priests dedicated to the work of God and the temple.

The New Testament Priesthood

God is seeking Spirit-filled priests to serve Him day and night before His throne. But now that Jesus has shed His blood to bring us near to God, we no longer need Levitical priests to mediate.

We offer our own sacrifices. Instead of flesh and blood, however, we offer sacrifices of worship, good works, and praise. Not just daily, weekly, or monthly, but continually throughout the day (Hebrews 13:15). Instead of going to the temple, we worship one on one, right here, wherever we are. How different from the Old Testament regimen!

Many of us may not feel worthy to be priests before God, but we are worthy because Jesus made us worthy. Even so, it's always good to approach God with a deep sense of humility. God does not despise a broken and contrite heart (Psalm 51:17). In fact, He looks favorably upon one who is of poor and contrite spirit and who trembles at His Word (Isaiah 66:2).

I really wonder how many of us fit that description? I wonder how many of us really care whether or not God esteems us? Are we so caught up in our own little finite worlds that God's perspective about our state of affairs is of no consequence to us? Once we understand that we are priests, this should enlarge our perspective because we are commissioned to care about His things.

It also matters not what we offer but how we offer it. Are we offering in faith? Are we seeking God's interests first or seeking things for our own benefit? In Isaiah 66:3, nkjv, God rejected the sacrifices offered by Israel's priesthood because they were being offered improperly:

> *"He who kills a bull is as if he slays a man; he who sacrifices a lamb, as if he breaks a dog's neck; he who offers a grain offering, as if he offers swine's blood; he who burns incense, as if he blesses an idol. Just as they have chosen their own ways, and their soul delights in their abominations."*

God does have a perspective, whether we admit it or not, and we had better pay attention to it. He scrutinizes and tests the motives of each heart to confirm and approve our actions. It is not good enough to just do right. We must do it for the right reasons, as well. The quality of our eternity is at stake. Moses warns us to see our life's end and be wise and to number our days (Psalm 90:12). The New Testament calls it "redeeming the time" for the days are evil (Ephesians 5:16, kjv).

Our time to do good is short.

Priests Intercede for the People

Aside from making sacrifices, another role played by priests is interceding for others through prayer. But unlike priests in the Old Testament, who offered up different types of prayer in accordance with the Law, we offer the prayers of our own hearts. In Revelation, we read that those prayers come up before God as the smell of incense on His altar (Revelation 5:8, 8:3,4). Hopefully, the sweet-smelling kind!

In Hebrews 4:16, we are invited to come boldly before the throne of grace, especially in our time of need. We are to offer all types of prayers—requests, confessions, thanks, praise, worship, and intercession to name a few. We are to pray in Jesus' name.

Christ not only encouraged us in this but commanded it, saying, "Until now you have not asked for anything in my name. Ask and you will receive and your joy will be complete" (John 16:24). Jesus says we can ask for anything and He will give it to us. For this to happen, we must ask in accordance with God's will.

Many call this concept "the priesthood of believers." It is a well accepted and understood biblical truth. Alas, many in the faith do not realize that they are priests and think the only priests operating today are clergy. This is far from what the Bible teaches. As believers, we are all priests and meant to intercede for others for the Kingdom's sake.

Man's traditions and ways are not God's ways. They often prevent us from understanding our role and function with the Almighty.

There are well-meaning believers that believe that we are to go through Mary to get to God. This is a well-meaning and understandable misperception because

Mary was a chosen and special vessel that God used to His glory.

However, 1 Timothy 2:5 clearly teaches that there is only one mediator between God and men—Christ Jesus. This verse alone should dispel the misconception that Mary or any believer is a go-between or mediator between us and God.

It is true, however, that in the Old Testament, the Jews did need a mediator, a Levitical priest, to intercede for them. In fact, the Jews were not even allowed into the inner part of the temple, where the worship of God was conducted.

But when Jesus died on the cross, the veil separating the Holy of holies (or the holiest, innermost part of the sanctuary) from the the outer part of the sanctuary was ripped from top to bottom, signifying that there no longer needed to be a separation between God and man.

Today, Jesus Himself serves as our High Priest (Hebrews 4:14), giving us direct access to the throne room of God!

The High Priest and the Holy of Holies

To better understand what a profound change it is to now have "broadband" access to God because of Jesus' blood, it helps to understand a little more about the temple.

Only the high priest could go into the Holy of holies, and only on Yom Kippur, the Day of Atonement. This was the day that the high priest would atone for the sins of the people for the year. He would ask forgiveness for himself, his family, and the nation of Israel, in that order.

If God heard him, and the priest survived with an acceptable blood sacrifice (if the sacrifice was not acceptable, the priest risked his life by dishonoring the Lord), then the forgiveness was secured.

Every year, this ritual had to be repeated in order for the people to be forgiven. It was a foreshadowing of another whom Isaiah said would come with a more long-lasting sacrifice for our iniquities and trespasses.

This was to be the purpose of the Messiah sent from God, who would accomplish atonement once and for all.

Great High Priest

The Bible tells us that Jesus' sacrificial death on the cross split the veil between the Holy Place and the Holy of holies— literally tore the thick curtain all the way down—signifying that we can now come into the private place where God dwells.

We have direct access by faith to a new and living way (Hebrews 10:20), opened by Jesus' flesh being broken for us on the cross. What is this new and living way? It is spiritual intimacy and oneness with God as He now indwells us by His Spirit.

Jesus not only acted as our High Priest in bringing the acceptable sacrifice for sins to God (Hebrews 7:23–28), but this sacrifice was proven acceptable to God and demonstrated as such by Jesus' rise from the dead. This is confirmed by Hebrews 10:12, which says, "But when this priest had offered for all time one sacrifice for sins, he sat down at the right hand of God."

As we continue reading, in verses 19–22 of the same chapter, we are encouraged to consider our place in all this.

> *Therefore, brothers, since we have confidence to enter the Most Holy Place by the blood of Jesus, by a new and living way opened for us through the curtain, that is, his body, and since we have a great priest over the house of God, let us draw near to God with a sincere heart in full assurance of faith, having our hearts sprinkled to cleanse us from a guilty conscience and having our bodies washed with pure water.*

In other words, let's take advantage of this miracle that Jesus accomplished by drawing near to God. Let's not waste the opportunity!

Life-Changing Truths

There are two other truths from Hebrews that are very special to me and that I hope will be life-changing for you, too.

First, in Hebrews 7:16, it is evident that Jesus has an endless life. The niv translation says that Jesus has an indestructible life. He cannot die. Talk about a superhero!

Second, in verse 25, it says that Jesus is able to save us to the uttermost (kjv) if we come to God by Him because He lives to intercede for us. This is our example. Can we do any less for the ones we know? Often, the Spirit will put someone on my heart, but I am unsure why.

Later that day, that person will call to share with me the circumstance or difficulty they are going through. It is amazing that if you are willing to follow the Lord's example of intercession, the Spirit will give you insights in advance of the situation to prepare you to help someone in need.

Believe me, saints of the Most High God, this is the best news you will ever hear. No man could have made this up. God ordained this way for us to have a new life through Jesus Christ. This is who we are. Now we have the privilege of coming directly into God's presence and ministering to Him and to others through our priestly role.

Not sure how to act like a priest? Try this prayer: "Lord, I am a blood-bought saint, and now I see that I am a priest forever with You to minister before Your throne. Lord, this is grace that I greatly appreciate. Nothing of me deserves this priesthood, but I commit to walking worthy of this call. Please help me minister to You and to others as Your will demands." All of these truths are surely amazing. But the amazing truths don't end here. Not only does the Word say that we are priests, but we are also members of one body.

13

members of one body

One of God's desires is to show His multi-dimensional wisdom to the heavenlies through the Body of Christ, also called the Church (Ephesians 3:10). Jesus is the Head and CEO of this body, so as believers, part of our spiritual identity is as part of this body, both corporately and locally.

Every believer throughout time—past, present, and future—is part of the universal Church. However, it is through the local body of believers, living and worshipping together, that we really learn to function as a unit, using our various gifts to accomplish a larger goal.

While many believers see their faith as a private thing, God sees it differently. When we are saved, we are not only saved from something—eternal hell—but we are saved into something, the Church. While there is much to say about the Church and our role within it, in the context of our spiritual identity, I want to focus on the concept of being "one" with other Christians.

I believe the key to unlocking and unleashing the power of the Church is Jesus' prayer in John 17:20-23:

> *My prayer is not for them alone. I pray also for those who will believe in me through their message, that all of them may be one, Father, just as you are in me*

and I am in you. May they also be in us so that the world may believe that you have sent me. I have given them the glory that you gave me, that they may be one as we are one: I in them and you in me. May they be brought to complete unity to let the world know that you sent me and have loved them even as you have loved me.

If we commit to fulfilling that prayer individually, then the Church corporately will accomplish its mission. We will fulfill our spiritual identity, both individually and corporately, as the glorious sons and daughters of God.

Oneness

What does it mean to "be one" or to have "oneness" in the Body of Christ? It is always good to see how the Bible defines such words, but to keep it simple, we will rely on a famous American who was a strong believer with a gift for definitions.

Oneness (wun'nis) n. 1. Singleness or unity 2. Agreement; concord 3. Sameness; identity. —Webster's Dictionary

This definition is a good start for what we need to learn and apply. "Oneness" implies that one or more individuals have unified for some cause. It is true that you are an individual, but the Bible says that apart from Christ, you can do nothing.

The independent life does not accomplish much for eternity. You need someone else with whom to unite to accomplish God's goals.

There is a great example of this that is familiar to us all. Can you guess what it is? The Trinity: Father, Son, and Holy Spirit. The three persons of the triune God are an awesome pattern of oneness in character, purpose, and direction.

Can you see the Father and Son not unifying over a decision? Or the Holy Spirit arguing with Jesus about a task that needs to be done? How ridiculous the thought is!

Believers need to unite in the same spirit, goal, and purpose. Each of us has different skills and gifts, but as we discussed in Chapter 11, there is a diversity of gifts, but only one ministry—the ministry of the Holy Spirit. Each of us is laboring individually to accomplish a larger goal.

A good word picture to describe how God intends us to function is the wheel within a wheel in the book of Ezekiel. The components of the two intersecting wheels were different, but they always tracked in the same direction perfectly, up and down and from side to side (Ezekiel 1:16–21).

Lessons from Babel

Ironically, one of the greatest lessons in oneness in the Bible comes from a group of people God ultimately judged because of that unity. In Genesis 11, we read of the incredible thing that happened at the plain of Shinar. At that time, there was only one language and one common speech, and while God had told mankind to scatter over all the earth, to fill it and be fruitful, the people chose instead to gather together and build a city to see what they could accomplish.

Not only did the people decide to build a city, but they decided to build a tower all the way to heaven. I am not sure why they wanted to do this. Wikipedia records several possibilities. One is that they were constructing the Tower as a welcome for their other Gods (they were called temple-towers).

Another possibility is that they were preparing in case God flooded the earth again. [3] After all, mankind has a pattern of doing their own thing, even (and sometimes especially!) when it is against God's will.

This first-ever skyscraper was quite an undertaking, and the people organized themselves with skill, ingenuity, and hard work. It was such an impressive project that God Himself decided to inspect the quality of their workmanship.

They not only passed the inspection, but God could see that without His personal and immediate intervention, they would succeed in their prideful endeavor. He basically said, "They build as one man. If we don't do anything, they will succeed and nothing will be impossible for them" (Genesis 11:6).

You know the rest of the story. God confused their speech by multiplying their languages. People could no longer understand one another and left off building the tower and the city. From there, they were scattered throughout the whole earth, which was God's original intention anyway.

The story of the Tower of Babel illustrates what the Bible calls the flesh. The result of this prideful, fleshly effort was that God punished mankind by scattering them to the four winds and creating nations with geographic boundaries.

The lesson I want to impart here is this: If unified flesh can accomplish anything apart from God's interference, how much more can unified spirit accomplish through oneness?

I say that those people can accomplish more than anything. Nothing on heaven or earth will be impossible for them. This kind of oneness is not possible to achieve on our own. Only the Spirit can accomplish complete oneness, and only through crucified believers, or those who keep their eyes on the Lord.

Agreement/Concord

Amos 3:3 asks, "Do two walk together unless they have agreed to do so?" The answer is that they cannot. And yet, saints, that is exactly what we are trying to do all the time.

We are attempting to walk together, to work together, to pray together, and to live life together, without doing it in agreement.

This is why we are failing and as weak as the world in our efforts. If we are not in agreement with God, it is to our loss. We disagree with things that we do not even understand.

Just as Jude says, men slander celestial beings that are more powerful than they are (Jude 8-10). When this realization hit me, it cut me to the heart. If we are not crying out with the Lord for agreement, then we are off track, living by the law of the world.

It is easy to live by the law of the flesh—or what we can see, taste, touch, and handle—and when we do, the grace of our God and Savior has eluded us.

It is also easy to be living in the flesh, but think we are living by the spirit. How to tell the difference? Let God put you to the test. Are you united in heart and spirit with the believers around you? If not, you fail the test of Jesus' high priestly prayer.

You may say, "Come on, Larry. Did He expect us to really be one in the spirit?" You bet He did. He was betting all eternity on this fact. Paul reiterates this principle in 1 Corinthians 1:10: "I appeal to you brothers, in the name of our Lord Jesus Christ, that all of you agree with one another, so that there may be no divisions among you and that you may be perfectly united in mind and thought."

Yet how can this be possible? Even among believers, we all have different personalities, skills, goals, desires, and needs. How can unity in this environment be achieved? Let me offer you three principles of grace that will help.

Three Principles of Grace

Grace Principle #1

Never disagree with another believer at the outset. If you feel that there is an error in their thinking or judgment, never tell them right away that you disagree. Instead, suggest that you talk about the issue and appeal to them from God's Word. Through fellowship and prayer, strive to come to an agreement in the spirit over whatever the issue might be.

When I say, "never disagree," I don't mean that you should act like robots and decide to have the same opinion on everything. But when you are quick to say, "I disagree," you are setting up a relationship based on antagonism because you are trying to impose your view on the other person.

Most people won't receive that spirit very well. Instead, enter into a discussion based on prayer and fellowship, which, rather than causing antagonism, tends to cause people to feel loved, included, and secure.

Sometimes, disagreements will be over something with a clear right and wrong, such as certain doctrinal issues that should not be under debate. But most times, disagreements occur over things without clear-cut answers, such as family decisions or the direction of a ministry. This is why it's so important to know the mind of God. In these cases, there are scriptural principles that you can use to help you in your decision.

Disunity has no place in the Body of Christ. With whomever you have a spirit of disagreement, you cannot walk, work, pray, or live. This is a huge cause of church splits, divorce, and relationship conflicts. Through fellowship and prayer, and knowing the mind of God, unity and agreement can usually be reached quickly—often within hours—if both parties are committed to finding a resolution.

Grace Principle #2

To agree with others, you must humble yourself before the Lord and submit to others out of reverence for Christ. Read 1 Peter 5. In this passage, we read that God opposes the proud but gives grace to the humble (verse 5). Later in the text, it speaks of suffering as a way to teach us this principle.

This seems to be the only way we learn to humble ourselves. Even Jesus was perfected in His obedience through His suffering.

What does this have to do with oneness? The only way we can achieve oneness is through humility. We all compete for ideas and goals. We can't all get our way. If you maintain a spirit of disagreement with someone, then you are prideful, plain and simple—determined to get your own way.

A better approach is for the two of you to pray together and humble yourselves before the Lord. If you do, it will not take long to agree.

This doesn't mean that you will always come to an agreement. If one or the other of the parties does not want to come to an agreement, then no agreement will be reached. But when both parties have a genuine desire to come into unity, it's amazing how quickly a resolution can be achieved.

When seeking agreement through the Spirit, remember that the Holy Spirit doesn't always think like you do. Walking in the Spirit means that you are willing to do things His way, even when it's different from yours.

This may mean that the other person bends to your will. It may also mean that you bend your will to theirs. Or perhaps the Holy Spirit has a compromise in mind—or even something completely different than either one of you is considering.

But you'll only find out through fellowship, seeking God, and prayer. You certainly won't uncover the will of the Holy Spirit through disunity and disagreement. I humbly implore leaders not to use forceful or manipulative methods to gain consensus, either. Take time to appeal and implore others from a stance of patient instruction.

This is why it is not possible to have oneness or be perfected in oneness without learning how to submit ourselves to one another. Jesus is the only CEO of the Church. Those who cannot submit to one another are walking in the flesh. We cannot be overcomers without learning to submit ourselves to one another.

Grace Principle #3

Regard no man according to the flesh. God does not look at the outward things but at the heart. He judges our worth not by our money, our standing in the community, or how well connected we are in the church, but by our brokenness and obedience. His Spirit will help us to look at each other in that way, as well. He can help us discern what is there and patiently deal with each situation.

God is true to His Word. He is watching to see if we can agree. Two people who can agree in the spirit can overthrow the gates of hell and take over any place they lay the soles of their feet.

Jesus was always in agreement with the Father. Where do you think He is now? He is at the right hand of majesty. When we, as believers, are in agreement, we also take our place in the heavens. Oh, saints, don't you see? There needs to be a willingness to let your flesh be slain for the glory of God, to be crucified so that we can agree with God.

High Priestly Prayer

With all of these principles in mind, let's look at Jesus' unity prayer again:

> *My prayer is not for them alone. I pray also for those who will believe in me through their message, that all of them may be one, Father, just as you are in me and I am in you. May they also be in us so that the world may believe that you have sent me. I have given them the glory that you gave me, that they be one as we are one. I in them and you in me. May they be brought to complete unity to let the world know that you sent me and have loved them even as you have loved me. (John 17:20–23)*

There is a reason Jesus prayed this way. He knew that the oneness He had with the Father meant everything to His life, ministry, death, and resurrection. He trusted His Father completely in all things.

Do you trust the Father in all things? We know that Jesus did everything He saw His Father doing (John 5:19). We know He spoke only what He heard His Father speak (John 8:28). We know that He walked in the power of the Spirit (Luke 4:14). We also know that

He is the Godhead in bodily form (see 1 Timothy 3:16, Philippians 2:6, especially kjv).

Now in the last prayer He would utter in front of His disciples before His agonizing death, Jesus zeroed in on the most important thing we could do to help Him. This is to be "one" just as He and the Father are one. When we allow ourselves to be perfected in this oneness (verse 23), the result is astounding. The entire world will know that the Father sent the Son—that His gospel message is true.

This is why Jesus did not pray that believers find gorgeous facilities in which to worship or unique names for their congregations. Rather, His prayer was for the world to be won through the example of believers walking in unity in spirit and truth.

The lone ranger, evangelist approach does not cut it. The world needs to be convinced of Jesus by the spirit of glory, love, submission, and committed sacrifice of His children. "By this all men will know that you are my disciples, if you love one another." (John 13:35)

Until this transpires, Jesus will weep over His Church as He did over Jerusalem. He is seeking a few true believers who will fulfill His prayer. Will you make that commitment in the town, city, or region you live in?

If you do, you will not only be walking in unity, but you will be given another privilege to be aware of, as well. You are His temples.

14

temples

Do you not know that your body is a temple of the Holy Spirit, who is in you, whom you have received from God? You are not your own; you were bought at a price. Therefore, honor God with your body. (1 Corinthians 6:19,20)

This is an amazing truth. Every person who is a believer in Jesus is God's temple. God wants to fill us with Himself, with His nature and divine attributes. This starts with His very presence, resident not just in our hearts and minds, but in our very bodies.

When we accept Jesus Christ as Lord and Savior, He enters our hearts, through His Spirit, and He brings with Him enough provisions for staying the rest of our lives.

This alone should make it clear why true believers undergo a transformation when they receive Jesus Christ as Savior and Lord. God Himself is living within us. Something fresh and new takes place when God enters a life. He doesn't just hang around, enjoying the view. He brings with Him a holy broom and starts cleaning house!

God wants to use each one of us, just as He designed us. Each of us has good works that we were created to perform and in which to walk from the foundation of the world.

> *For we are God's workmanship, created in Christ Jesus to do good works, which God prepared in advance for us to do. (Ephesians 2:10)*

God also wants to inhabit and fill His temple as He did in days of old. He wants this temple to be clean—free from sin—and useful for the purposes He has in mind.

Shadow of Things to Come

The Jerusalem Temple built by the Israelites had three major facilities: the outer court, the inner court, and the Holy of holies. The Holy of holies was the inner sanctum where the Ark of the Covenant (a solid gold chest) resided.

The Ark held several items: the Ten Commandments, tablets of stone inscribed by the very finger of God; a jar with a sample of the manna (bread) that God used to feed to the Israelites in the wilderness; and Aaron's staff, which miraculously budded with flowers to show where and on whom God's authority rested during the establishment of Israel.

With the resurrection of Jesus, God has moved His residence from this building to the hearts of men. Our hearts have become the Holy of holies. Instead of the Ten Commandments, we have Jesus, who is the end of the law (Romans 10:4) for all who believe.

Instead of the manna from the wilderness, we have the Bread of Life—the Living Manna (John 6:58). Instead of the budding staff, we have the True Shepherd (John

10:11), who holds the authoritative staff and transfers that authority to us (Matthew 28:18).

Remember, the Lord does not come to take sides, but to take over. He wants us to receive Him as He really is—the Lord of Glory.

An important part of the Ark was the two seraphim, one at each end. These angel-like beings were hammered from solid gold, like the rest of the Ark, and faced one another with their wings extended, touching at the center.

Between the seraphim was "the mercy seat," or the place where God's Shekinah glory—the Spirit of His presence— shined forth. Does this sound like a scene from a movie?

Better than the movies is real life, life in Christ. Now, that Shekinah glory shines forth from our hearts and lives as a testimony that we are in the age of grace, where God dwells with man by His Spirit.

God offers us the privilege of housing Him through the Spirit in our hearts, by faith. Are you the landlord or the tenant of your body?

Although it might seem as though we invite the Spirit in as a tenant, the reverse is actually true. God is the landlord. We are just renting.

Worship: Any Place, Anytime

As God's temple, what should we look like? A temple is a place of worship, a place of peace. It is a place where God is lifted up and exalted to His proper position. With God physically dwelling within us, not one of us has to go anywhere to enter into worship. We worship right where we are, because wherever we are, God is, too. This is an astounding biblical truth that is part of the fabric of our spiritual identity.

How should this affect our daily lives? As God's temple, we are to be in a perennial state of worship: at home, in the car, at school, at work, with our friends, at the movies, waiting in line for the transit bus. That worship is reflected in our words, our attitudes, our actions, and our praise. What does your temple look like?

With this in mind, two New Testament lessons, the Samaritan woman at the well and the parable of the vine and the branches, make more sense than ever before.

Let's start with the Samaritan woman. In John 4, we read that, while waiting for His disciples to return with supplies, Jesus met a Samaritan woman.

Against all cultural stigma of His day, Jesus engaged her in conversation by asking for a drink from the well from which she was preparing to draw water. He quickly turned the conversation from water to spiritual matters, challenging the woman's understanding.

One of the religious debates of that day was where the people should worship, whether at the Jewish temple in Jerusalem or there, in Samaria, where the woman dwelled.

The conversation picks up in verse 20:

> *"Our fathers worshipped on this mountain, but you Jews claim that the place where we must worship is in Jerusalem." Jesus then declared, "Believe me, woman, a time is coming when you will worship the*

> *Father neither on this mountain nor in Jerusalem... Yet a time is coming and has now come when the true worshipers will worship the Father in spirit and truth, for they are the kind of worshipers the Father seeks. God is spirit, and his worshipers must worship in spirit and in truth."* (John 4:20–24)

The place in which we worship simply does not matter to God. What matters is that the Holy Spirit and truth be central to our worship. It speaks to this in the scriptures, when it says, "Lord, you have been our dwelling place throughout all generations" (Psalm 90:1).

In other words, if we dwell in God—and now, in this age of grace, Jesus dwells in us—we are in the right place. This is precisely what Jesus was explaining in the parable of the vine and branches:

"If a man remains in me and I in him, he will bear much fruit; apart from me you can do nothing" (John 15:5). It is important to God that we dwell and abide in each other and that the union is secure.

Who's Living in Me?

This starts with the understanding that God now indwells the believer through His promised Holy Spirit. Jesus gives us this promise in John 14:23,26:

> *"We will come to him and make our home with him. But the Counselor, the Holy Spirit, whom the Father will send in my name, will teach you all things and will remind you of everything I have said to you."*

As recorded in Acts 19, when the Apostle Paul was on his way to Ephesus, he comes across a group of believers who held a misconception about their faith. He asks them:

> *"Did you receive the Holy Spirit when you believed?" They answered, "No, we have not even heard that there is a Holy Spirit." So Paul asked, "Then what baptism did you receive?" "John's baptism," they replied. Paul said, "John's baptism was a baptism of repentance. He told the people to believe in the one coming after him – that is, in Jesus." On hearing this, they were baptized into the name of the Lord Jesus. When Paul placed his hands on them, the Holy Spirit came on them, and they spoke in tongues and prophesied. There were about twelve men in all. (Acts 19:2–7)*

Although the New Testament refers to these twelve as disciples, they still did not understand who the Holy Spirit was or His role in their lives. Even two thousand years later, our teaching is not adequate concerning the indwelling Holy Spirit—His role, His function, and His vital importance to every believer.

The Holy Spirit is God living in you and me, with God's personality, mind, and attributes. Do you think that the Holy Spirit has the ability to speak to you? To teach you all things? To enact amazing miracles through you? You'd better because it's true!

Vessels and Instruments

We are vessels, channels, and instruments in His hands. We must learn to let God's Spirit flow freely through us, getting to know Him as intimately as possible so we will trust His leading.

After all, making Jesus Lord of our lives is not something to be taken lightly. When we accept Him into our hearts, we are making a commitment. If we take that commitment for granted, if we remain carnal, focused on the appetites of our bodies, and ceasing to be useful to God, He has no obligation to give us long, fruitful lives. Consider the story of Ananias and Sapphira, who lied to the Holy Spirit and fell down dead (Acts 5:1–11).

One person explained the phenomena of the indwelling like our bodies being "God bottles" that contain God. One does not sit there, staring at a Coke bottle, amazed at its beauty. One drinks the soda pop and throws out the bottle after the soda has been drunk. If we have been slothful in our relationship to God and have made His indwelling of no effect, our bottle is in danger of being useless and thrown away. This is a humbling thought!

Jesus Himself gave a similar example, using salt. He said that, if salt loses its saltiness, it is good only to be thrown away (Matthew 5:13). Therefore, we must make every day count for eternity.

God has an expectation that we live useful and productive lives. Scripture is clear that, if we neglect our salvation and the God who redeemed us, He will continue to reach out, reach out, and reach out, trying to wake us up from our spiritual stupor. But if we continually resist the Holy Spirit and our testimony becomes harmful—rather than useful— sometimes God will discipline us unto death (1 John 5:16).

Our usefulness is tested according to the principle that Paul shared with the Corinthians: "You should be looking at yourselves to make sure that you are really

Christ's. It is yourselves that you should be testing. You ought to know by this time that Christ Jesus is in you unless you are not real Christians at all." (2 Corinthians 13:5–6, j.b. phillips)

I want to summarize the biblical truth that our bodies are God's temple.

> *For we, remember, are ourselves temples of the living God, as God has said: I will dwell in them and walk in them. (2 Corinthians 6:16, j.b. phillips)*

> *"Do you not know that your body is a temple of the Holy Spirit, who is in you, whom you have received from God? You are not your own; you were bought at a price. Therefore, honor God with your body." (1 Corinthians 6:19,20)*

The second passage is written in the context of the need to avoid sexual immorality. We are meant to have sexual intercourse with whomever the Lord brings to us within the loving confines of monogamous marriage. Whoever we have sexual intercourse with, we become one with.

We understand from the scriptures that sex within marriage is designed to help us understand that we were also meant for spiritual intercourse with God. Is there a more intimate way for God to fellowship with us than to indwell and be with us forever?

When God enters us, we become holy and righteous.

15

holy and righteous

For just as through the disobedience of the one man, the many were made sinners, so also through the obedience of the one man the many will be made righteous. (Romans 5:19)

For he chose us in him before the creation of the world to be holy and blameless in his sight. (Ephesians 1:4) God's Word teaches that every believer is holy and righteous. It does not say that we are holy and righteous in ourselves. It says we are holy and righteous because God has made us this way. These concepts must be firmly planted in our hearts if we are to understand our true spiritual identity.

As believers, our fundamental nature is now identified with God and His Spirit. Therefore, it should not surprise you that God identifies us this way. It is not as though anyone earns this status, as if our works could do that for us.

Rather, our spiritual identity, by grace, is now wrapped up in God's very person. Since that divine power now lives in us, we are, in a very real sense, holy.

It does not mean that we are morally perfect like God or that we are sinless. God alone is in that category. But we are associated with the divine person and strive to live holy lives by the power of God.

To many, this may seem impossible. But possible it is. The Bible declares it. The two most common words for "holy" applied to believers in the New Testament are holios and hagios. Holios literally means "consecrated" and "associated with the divine character."

Hagios means "sacred," "pure," and "blameless." So when God declares us "holy," that is exactly how He sees us. And as holy ones, we are to live that way, as well.

Some may respond to this declaration by saying, "If only I had more strength to resist sin" or "If only I were around the right ministry or church, maybe I could live more holy than I do now." This totally misses the point of who we are in Christ.

In 2 Peter 1:3,4, Peter declares that, as partakers of the divine nature, we have everything we need for life and godliness. That means right here and right now. We do not have to do anything to be holy. We already are holy. We merely have to rest in this biblical truth.

I know this is too wonderful to believe. But believe me, dear saint, it is true. You may not always live like you are holy, but you are holy, no matter how you may feel about yourself.

Here is another truth almost too wonderful to believe. If you receive this truth, your behavior will conform to your belief. The Spirit in you will bring His thoughts to bear on your life to convict you of sin and enable you to repent and become the person God intends for you to be. He makes everything beautiful in its time (Ecclesiastes 3:11).

Spiritual Inheritance

How can all of this be true? Simple. When we receive Jesus as Lord and Savior, His righteousness is given to us. It's like receiving an inheritance. When someone passes away and wills you a sum of money, you receive the money, not because you've earned it, but because it is the will of the one who died that you should have it. It becomes yours through no effort of your own.

So it is with Jesus' righteousness. When we accept Jesus as Lord, He gives us His righteousness. We don't earn it. It is simply ours. When God looks at us, He does not see our earthly righteousness or the righteousness we deserve in ourselves, but only the perfect righteousness of Christ.

Put another way, because Jesus is righteous, His righteousness is imputed to us through our faith in His death for our sins. "To impute" is an accounting term that indicates a credit being applied to an account. 2 Corinthians 5:21 sums it up well:

> *"God made Him who had no sin to become sin for us so that in Him we might become the righteousness of God."*

Unbelievable! We have become the righteousness of God.

Repeat this to your inner man over and over again. Say, "I have become the righteousness of God." With this foundation, let's look again at 1 John 3:7, kjv, that jewel of a verse: "He that doeth righteousness is righteous, even as He is righteous." No matter how we look at this verse—forward or backward—it is true either way.

Let's start with forward. A person who does righteous things is a righteous person. That is why he does righteous things. But that person's righteous deeds are not of himself.

Those deeds are only made possible because of the righteousness of Christ. He is the source of all righteousness. Now backward. Jesus is righteous. Based on His righteousness, we also have become the righteousness of God.

Now it is natural for us, as God's righteous children, to walk righteously before him. It makes sense forward, backward (or even sideways), fellow believer.

Living Up to Your Identity

You are holy and righteous. Instead of becoming proud of these biblical truths, however, we should be greatly humbled to realize what new creatures we have become. We are totally made of new stuff now. The heavenly DNA is taking hold of us and we are aliens of this world.

Once we are made righteous, we should naturally strive to live up to this identity, especially if we are living and walking in the Spirit.

If anyone has seen or read *The Cross and the Switchblade*, the story of evangelist David Wilkerson, he tells the story about how, early in his ministry, he was ministering to street gangs in New York. At a service, he took an offering and gave the responsibility of collecting the money to a gang leader named Nicky Cruz.

This young man had never been trusted before and was stunned that Wilkerson would entrust the collection to his care. This trust impelled Nicky to live up to that trust, so instead of stealing the money, he protected it. Ultimately, Nicky came to give his life to the Lord and became a powerful evangelist in his own right.

Knowing that we are holy and righteous in the eyes of God is not designed to make us spiritually lazy, but spiritually zealous. Knowing that God sees us as holy and righteous should cause us to want to live up to the identity that He has already provided for us.

Peter calls us "aliens" and "strangers" in this world (1 Peter 2:11). We have become a people set apart to call forth God's praises. This is a uniquely wonderful position, part of the calling of a holy people.

If we can commit ourselves to being who the Bible clearly says we are, we will easily do the things that we are supposed to do. Focus on being who you are meant to be.

Believe who you are! Then you will carry out God's will without fussing and fighting. I am not saying it will be easy, but if you rest in these truths, if you work out your salvation with fear and trembling, the Overcoming Christ will overcome all that is in your path. It is God who works in you, both to will and to do according to His good pleasure (Philippians 2:12,13).

Throughout the Bible, it is common for the scriptures to refer to unbelieving people as "sinners," but this was not the word the Bible uses to describe those who believe. This next chapter may surprise you as to how believers are described, and what a high calling we have to live up to.

16

saints

Now that Jesus has come to live in you (assuming He has) by His Spirit, how do you describe your true identity? In other words, who are you? If you say that you are a believer, a Christian (a "little Christ"), you are accurate from a biblical standpoint.

It is common to hear believers say that they are now children of God. After all, the Bible teaches it. You are either a believer and you belong to God or you are an unbeliever who belongs to Satan.

But did you know that you are either a sinner or a saint? Though we have heard the term "saint" before, we tend to identify more with being a sinner than a saint because we typically learn these terms in the context of religious and doctrinal teaching or have heard them used as clichés in everyday life.

It is important to understand the origin and the intent of these words as they are used in the Bible. As explained in Chapter 2, the word "sin" came from the sport of archery and signified completely missing the mark of the intended target. Thus, the term "sinner" is a biblical reference to a person whose life has completely missed the mark of God's intended purpose for their life.

Scripturally, the term is used synonymously with the term "unbeliever," indicating someone whose life is still under the control of Satan. Left to themselves, sinners have no chance of pleasing God.

Therefore, for a believer, it is a deception to think you are a sinner as part of your fundamental identity. By contrast, the term "saint" represents a sanctified person. One who is "called out." Being a saint is synonymous with being a believer.

Of course, through time, the term "saint" has been misconstrued to mean a perfect person with holy behavior who is honored after their death for some particular outstanding characteristic.

Consequently, the glory goes to men for their good works rather than to the Creator who made the good works possible through faith and grace in Jesus Christ.

It is important to understand that being a saint does not mean one has sinless behavior. If you say that you have not sinned, you make God out to be a liar (1 John 1:10). Being a saint reveals your identity as a believer, and there are inherent responsibilities in this identity to represent God in a glorifying way.

Who's Teaching You?

But aren't we just "sinners saved by grace"? We hear this a lot, and this is fine sounding theology taught by many of our pastors and favorite radio teachers. They teach that we have two natures within us, a sinful nature and a holy nature.

These two natures battle within us like two knights—one representing good and the other representing evil—and the holy nature ultimately wins the battle over the sinful one.

Is it true that you are a spiritual schizophrenic? Are there two natures battling within you for control? I think not. Though your flesh is warring against the Holy Spirit (as described in Chapter 10), you do not have a dual nature lingering within you.

You are God's temple (Chapter 14), a new creature (Chapter 8) who is dearly loved (Chapter 25). Before you were a Christian, your tendency was to "miss the mark" because of sin. Now you are able to hit the target that God desires for your life because He has regenerated you from the inside out. You are not a sinner anymore.

Consider this passage:

> *For it is time for judgment to begin with the family of God; and if it begins with us, what will the outcome be for those who do not obey the gospel of God? And, if it is hard for the righteous to be saved, what will become of the ungodly and the sinner? (1 Peter 4:17,18)*

Did you see it? In these verses—as well as the other verses like them—the word "righteous" is used synonymously with "believer." And the words "ungodly" and "sinner" are used synonymously with "unbeliever." Let's look at some more.

Therefore the wicked will not stand in the judgment, nor sinners in the assembly of the righteous. (Psalm 1:5)

If you consider yourself to be a sinner, then according to this verse, you will not stand in the congregation of the righteous. But according to scripture, this is exactly where all believers will be!

Do not take away my soul along with sinners or my life with bloodthirsty men. (Psalm 26:9)

If you are a believer, then your life (in an eternal sense) cannot be taken away because you have eternal life. Unbelievers or sinners, however, can have their lives taken away.

Then I will teach transgressors your ways and sinners will turn back to you. (Psalm 51:13)

Here, David is speaking of reaching out to unbelievers and helping them come to God through faith and repentance. As in the passages above, the Bible is using the term to refer to unbelievers.

Listen to 1 John 3:9-10 in the kjv:

"Whosoever is born of God doth not commit sin; for his seed remaineth in him: and he cannot sin, because he is born of God. In this the children of God are manifest, and the children of the devil: whosoever doeth not righteousness is not of God, neither he that loveth not his brother."

This passage is not saying that believers never commit sin. But in Greek (the language in which most of the

New Testament was originally written), the verb tense for "sin" here indicates a continuing action.

It is not talking about believers not committing any sin at all, but rather, exhibiting a pattern of behavior—a lifestyle. In other words, believers do not continue in their pattern of sinning. They stop, repent, and do what is right.

New Look at Your Identity

This passage is my trump card from the Lord to you. Believers do not casually and naturally commit sin. Why? Because God's seed is inside them. And what is God's seed? The Holy Spirit, of course.

Once we become a friend of the Lord, it is no longer natural for us to sin. If your identity is in Christ, then the Holy Spirit is in you and you are born of God.

This Spirit will never cause, tempt, or provoke you to sin. On the contrary, the Spirit hates sin. His job is to guide you into all truth (John 16:13)—and that means guiding you away from sin.

Can you separate your spirit from God's? No. 1 Corinthians 2:12-16 says some important things about the Spirit. Please read these passages carefully. You have a powerful person dwelling in you. You have the mind of Christ. Not the carnal, fleshly mind that used to bring deception and death.

You may want to stop here to rejoice and thank God for what He has done in you. Tell him that you believe that you have the mind of Christ (1 Corinthians 2:16).

The devil's work is mainly deception. His prize is blood in his pockets, especially the blood of God's saints. If you see yourself as a sinner, you have been deceived by his lie that you are inherently sinful. This is a deception intended to disrupt the intimacy you have with your Heavenly Father.

As a Christian, at the core of your identity, you are not a sinner at all. I am not saying that you do not sin. I am saying that, by the Bible's definition, sinners are unbelievers.

Therefore, according to the Word of God, you are not a sinner.

If Not Sinners, Then What?

If we aren't sinners, who are we? We are righteous in Christ (see Chapter 15). This righteousness is not based on our works but upon our faith in Christ. Over and over, the Bible says that believers are righteous. Do you believe that?

You should. Righteousness is a question of your fundamental identity. Look again at the passage in 1 John 3. Righteous actions flow from a righteous person. Out of your mouth, you speak what is in your heart. A righteous man speaks out of the good stored up in him (Matthew 12:35, Luke 6:45). And whatever you store up inside you is directly related to what you think about.

This is why we are told to think about things that are true, noble, right, pure, lovely, admirable, excellent, and praiseworthy (Philippians 4:8). But if you do not see yourself as righteous, your thoughts will ever be swimming downstream in the muck.

Here are two more examples that prove your identity is in righteousness:

> *And these [unbelievers] will go away into everlasting punishment, but the righteous into eternal life." (Matthew 25:46, kjv)*

> *For as by one man's disobedience many were made sinners, so by the obedience of one shall many be made righteous. (Romans 5:19)*

In another place, Jesus says that He calls, not the righteous, but the sinners to repentance (Luke 5:32). The righteous do not need to repent to eternal life. You can only receive eternal life once. Only a sinner still needing the life of God in him can repent this way.

In another example, in John 9:31, the blind man states that God does not listen to sinners. He listens to the godly man who does His will. Again, this is not so much speaking of individual actions, but to our spiritual identity.

God does not hear an unbeliever's prayer the same way He hears a believer's prayer. To the believer, there is a promise of an answer to the one who prays in Christ's name, according to His will (John 16:24). The unbeliever has no such assurance.

There is a sense in which God is plugging His ears with His fingers, saying, "You are not coming in the right way through My Son, so I will not pay attention."

Finally, let's look at the famous salvation passage in Romans 5:8: "But God demonstrates his love for us, yet while we were still sinners, Christ died for us." We were indeed sinners, but now we are light in the world. We are righteous, not because of our own behavior, but by God's transforming identity. The key to being transformed in your spiritual identity is to believe God at His Word.

No Longer Objects of Wrath

As previously stated, God says that we were, by nature, objects of wrath. What are we after salvation regeneration? We are no longer objects of wrath. That is reserved for the ungodly and the sinner.

We are God's legitimate children, and consequently, are objects of blessing, affection, loving discipline (Hebrews 12: 5-11), and God-ordained prosperous plans.

Jeremiah 29:11 changed my fear of death forever when the Holy Spirit showed me that God had only good intended for me.

> *"For I know the plans I have for you," declares the LORD, "plans to prosper you and not to harm you, plans to give you hope and a future."*

In all of the passages in the Bible that have the word "sinner" in them, only a few could be interpreted as having reference to believers. One such passage is 1 Timothy 1:15.

Another is James 4:8. In 1 Timothy 1:15, Paul calls himself "the chief of sinners." I have greatly struggled to understand why this might be an exception to the clear biblical distinction between a sinner and a saint.

So I looked at the context to see what heinous crime Paul had committed: none recently. He was referring back to his life before Christ when his life was stained with sin, including the martyring of Christian believers. Paul was still taking responsibility for a sin-stained past.

Paul had a humble, balanced view of who he was in Christ. Part of that balance was remembering who he used to be as a sinner. However, Paul also knew how to forget what was behind and press toward what was ahead.

There is a sense that the past is still part of us and that we are held accountable to the past. We will be called to account for our choices at the judgment seat of Christ (1 Corinthians 3:11–13).

Fortunately, by dying on the cross for our sins, Jesus took the sins of humanity upon His own body, and once believers receive this gift, God, through His grace, casts our sin as far as the east is from the west (Psalm 103:12).

When we enter eternity, we do not take our sins with us. Even so, we cannot claim that we did not commit sins or that our behavior had no effect on others. Instead, we learn from our mistakes and correct our behavior. But unbelievers do carry their sins and their eternal consequences with them.

The second of these references come from James 4:8:

"Wash your hands, you sinners, and purify your hearts, you double-minded."

James clearly spoke to believers. His language is tinged with irony. In other words, if we act like sinners when we are really saints, we are double-minded.

How is it that we act like sinners, who are not close to God, when, in fact, we are in His bosom? James exhorts believers to come "close to God and He will come close to you." Then he charges us to humble ourselves from pride so that God's grace will lift us up in due time.

When God lifts us up, we have the power, love, and Spirit-filled walk that are natural and befitting for the saint of God. Although we are declared righteous in the eyes of God, it is still important to have a balanced and a sober view of oneself.

Spiritual pride can get the best of us, even when we are trying to view ourselves from a biblical and right perspective. The point is simply that a "sinner" is the spiritual identity of an unbeliever. They are synonymous. Once you believe in the Son of God, you are no longer an unbeliever— you are no longer a sinner.

How you see yourself is important because one's actions tend to flow from one's view of self. If you think that you are a sinner (even if God doesn't see you this way), then sinful actions will follow. On the flip side, if you see yourself as righteous, you will tend act that way, too.

If you are not a sinner, are you really a saint? Yes, you are! In over 100 references to this term in the New Testament, everyone refers to a follower of God.

Just to drive home this point even further, let's try an experiment. If Christians really are sinners, as many believe, then we might interchange this term with the actual words used in the New Testament. If we do this, what do you think might happen?

"Behold the Lord cometh with his sinners" (1 Thessalonians 3:13, kjv). Hmmm… really? Is this what the verse says? "To the sinners in Ephesus…" (Ephesians 1:1).Yeah, right!

Believers are not referred to as sinners. In all of the books of the Bible that start with a greeting, the greeting goes to saints, never to sinners.

Or the popular spiritual tune rewrote: "Oh when the sinners come marching in! Oh when the sinners come marching in! Oh, Lord, I want to be in that number. When the sinners come marching in!" Ridiculous, of course. Sinners don't march in victory or return with the Lord in the air or represent the Church in the heavenly city.

A saint is a "called out one," a part of the one body—a holy, righteous lover of the Lord. This is saying nothing about our behavior. This is who we are. It is our identity.

The scriptures are replete with this type of language. But we prefer to sound religious in our self-abasing lingo, "We are sinners saved by grace." No, we are not! We were sinners saved by grace. Now we are light in the Lord.

The teaching that God's saints are "sinners" is man's doing—man's teaching. It has been wrought into the minds of believers, not to keep them humble, but to deceive them into discouraging and impotent thoughts.

The truth is that we have an awesome identity in Christ that is too wonderful to fully put into words. It is something that we must experience for ourselves in order to understand, and even then, it takes a lifetime.

This identity includes one more yet incomprehensible fact. God not only calls us saints, but He also calls us overcomers.

17

overcomers!

They overcame him by the blood of the lamb and by the word of their testimony. (Revelation 12:11)

The Bible is clear that we are to be overcomers. But what does that mean? What does being an overcomer look like in our daily lives? According to scripture, there appear to be three major categories that we need to overcome: the world, the flesh, and the devil.

About 15 years after I became a believer, and even after I had developed a good handle on my spiritual identity, I stopped short when reading John 16:33: "I have told you these things, so that in me you may have peace. In this world, you will have trouble. But take heart! I have overcome the world."

I read this verse over and over again. I knew that God was speaking to me, but I wrestled with what He was trying to say. Finally, I admitted, "I do not know what this means, Lord. Please show me." For four months, there was silence, but I continued to press in to understand.

Finally, the understanding came. It did not come to me through words, but through pictures in my mind—pictures of Jesus overcoming everything in the fleshly realm: overcoming people's lack of faith in Him;

overcoming the pain and shame of going to the cross; overcoming the lack of love in the world; overcoming the independent spirit in the world by constant fellowship with His Heavenly Father.

With this sudden burst of insight, I proclaimed, "I believe! I believe you are the overcomer of the world!" Jesus immediately replied, "Now that you believe, you are an overcomer of the world."

Overcoming the World

My conclusion is that to be an overcomer of the world, you must believe John 16:33. Jesus overcame the world.

Therefore, if we are to emulate Jesus, we are to overcome the world, too. This has proven difficult for many believers, but I am convinced that this is because most simply don't understand what it means to be overcomers—or even that we are supposed to be overcomers. Either this, or we are too busy having fellowship with the world to bother overcoming it.

So the first step in overcoming is renouncing and repenting of our love of the world. Just consider what God has to say about the love of the world:

> *Do not love the world or anything in the world. If anyone loves the world, the love of the Father is not in him. For everything in the world – the cravings of sinful man, the lust of his eyes and the boasting of what he has and does – comes not from the Father but from the world. The world and its desires pass away, but the man who does the will of God lives forever. (1 John 2:15–17)*

We have a tendency to love the world. But just as the scriptures are clear that we cannot love both God and money, we cannot love both the world and God. As believers in Jesus, we must learn to overcome the world, not embrace it.

You may not think you love the world, but let's consider these few examples:

Do you share the gospel with your neighbors? If not, why not? Are you afraid of what they might think? If so, then you love the approval of the world more than the things of God.

Is there a program on television that has content you know that God disapproves of, but you watch it anyway? If so, then you love the things of the world more than honoring your heavenly Father.

Do you work late, trying to achieve financial security, even though you know that your relationship with your wife and children is suffering? If so, then you love the security of the world more than you love the security provided by the great I AM.

Heart-Check Your Desires

Overcoming the world starts with realizing our own fears and desires. The Psalmist wrote:

> *"Delight yourself in the LORD and he will give you the desires of your heart" (Psalm 37:4)*

And in Matthew 6:18–33, Jesus talks about the natural fears that people have about meeting their material needs, but says that God knows that we have need of these things, so we should "seek first his kingdom and his righteousness, and all these things [food, shelter, and clothing] will be given to you as well."

There is an important principle in both of these verses. Seek first the kingdom of God, then your daily needs will be met. Delight in the Lord, then He will give you the desire of your heart. It all starts with doing His will first, ahead of your own.

When we do this, two things happen. First, we find that the things that we seek begin to change. So do our desires. God begins to conform our hearts to His, and our desires begin to change so that they reflect His perfect purpose and will. What a miracle!

Next, something even more amazing begins to happen. As our desires and motivations change, the pleasures and comforts of the world no longer have the same attraction and power over us. The things that were once yokes and bonds in our lives begin to break and we become free to live out our lives exactly as God planned. We have overcome the world!

How to get started? Neil Anderson suggests one very effective approach in his excellent book *The Bondage Breaker*. He uses the terms "renounce and announce":

1. Renounce any hint of worldly desires that you sense in yourself or that God's Spirit gently points out to you. Keep renouncing until there are no desires left to renounce.

2. Announce to the heavens and the world your true spiritual identity—that you are an overcomer of the world once and for all. This commitment must be

renewed as often as is necessary, particularly when you feel that worldly desires are motivating your heart and actions. You will see that your proclamation, by faith, will have the transforming effect that you are hoping for.

Remember that you are not overcoming the world by your own power or strength or by a sheer commitment to change. God expects every Christian to make progress and to become the overcomer that He designed them to be.

Therefore, because God never expects you to do anything without giving you the power to do it, it is His power you are drawing on, not your own.

This should be a great comfort to us since the tools we need are within the grasp of every believer: our faith and our belief in Jesus as the Son of God:

> *For everyone born of God overcomes the world. This is the victory that has overcome the world, even our faith. Who is it that overcomes the world? Only he who believes that Jesus is the Son of God. (1 John 5:4,5)*

Overcoming the Flesh

The next major area to overcome is the flesh, which is closely related to the world. We talked about the definition of the flesh in Chapter 10 (spiritual beings part 2), which laid a foundation for the difference between the flesh and the spirit.

The goal was to help you identify with (and live by) the Spirit of God rather than the flesh. Remember that the flesh represents the independent life, the self-life apart from God.

One of the most difficult things in the Christian life is to overcome one's own flesh. But remember that while the spirit is willing, the flesh is weak. The Holy Spirit is able to help us in our weakness (Romans 8:26). The Spirit is able to intercede for us. The Spirit is able to counsel us.

The Spirit is able to show us a way to escape in every situation (1 Corinthians 10:13). Not only that, but God's grace is sufficient for us to be overcomers of our flesh (2 Corinthians 12:9).

Jesus showed us an example. As a man, He faced the same temptations as we do—rejection, suffering, and death—yet He overcame them because He was set on doing His Father's will and everything necessary to accomplish that will.

While this may be difficult, we are given the power to overcome old patterns—old habits—and establish new ones.

> *Knowing this, that our old man is crucified with him, that the body of sin might be destroyed, that henceforth we should not serve sin. Let not sin therefore reign in your mortal body, that ye should obey it in the lusts thereof. (Romans 6:6,12, kjv)*

Our fleshly desires are closely related to the love of the world since the love of the world gives birth to those desires. Therefore, by applying the principles of living the spirit life (Chapters 9-10) and the principles of overcoming the world, we can overcome the flesh, as well.

The Devil

We have talked about two of the three major areas that need to be overcome as we develop our spiritual identity— the world and the flesh. The third major area to overcome is the devil.

> *I write to you young men, because you have overcome the evil one. I write to you dear children, because you have known the Father. I write you fathers, because you have known him who is from the beginning. I write to you young men, because you are strong, and the word of God lives in you, and you have overcome the evil one. (1 John 2:13,14)*

The Bible makes it clear that every believer has an enemy (see Chapter 21, "Satan's Adversaries"). In the scriptures, he is called by many names: Satan, the evil one, the devil, Beelzebub, the serpent, the prince of the power of the air, the god of this age, and more. It is his goal to stir up our fleshly desires, our love of the world, and through various deceptions, entice us away from the Kingdom of God.

Overcoming the devil starts by getting to know him. To the extent that we know him, we will be aware of his influence, his ways and tactics, and his power. Paul said that he was not unaware of the devil's schemes.

The devil is a master planner and an expert strategist. Left to ourselves, we will lose every time against him. He is smarter and stronger than we are, and he has resources to leverage against us. He is also the prince of perseverance. He can outlast every one of us.

Although I do not want to give Satan too much credit, I do not want to underestimate him, either.

Jesus Himself had to contend with Satan during His temptation in the wilderness (Matthew 4). Jesus was neither flippant nor hasty in His contest with Satan. He relied on the Word of God, and if we want to defeat the enemy of our soul, we must rely on the Word of God also.

Do not think that sheer desire or determination will be enough. Our weapons are not carnal, but spiritual for pulling down strongholds (2 Corinthians 10:3–5). We must employ the heavenly weapons given us for a sure victory.

One very important observation we can take from the spiritual contest between Jesus and Satan was that Satan went right to Jesus' identity—His spiritual identity. Twice, Satan taunted Jesus, saying, "If you are the Son of God..."

It is like saying, "Prove it! Show me that you really are who you say you are." Jesus did not need to prove Himself. He was secure in His spiritual identity. We must be secure in our spiritual identities, as well.

Dear saint of the Most High God, are you secure in who you are because Christ is in you? If not, the time will come when the devil will challenge and tempt you. Do not succumb to his deception and treachery. Resist the devil and he will flee from you. Humble yourselves before the Lord, and he will lift you up (James 4:7,10).

If deception is Satan's main tactic, then fear is his greatest weapon. Overcoming fear is all about building a strong relationship with Christ. It is an inward struggle, an inward challenge.

What causes fear? The scripture teaches us that God's love drives out fear (1 John 4:18). The revelation of God's love starts with understanding that we are forgiven. We have a clean slate. Our sins are dealt with once and for all, thanks to Jesus and His sacrificial death on the cross. We can keep short accounts with our Master if we do anything that displeases Him.

God has good planned for us (Jeremiah 29:11), not evil. He wants the best for each and every one of His children. If we are truly His followers, there is no punishment or condemnation awaiting us (Romans 8:1). We must believe this great news. We must embrace it. It must be a part of our very fabric.

This is our love for God: to believe what His Word says and not be given over to unbelief. Unbelief causes fear. When we overcome our fears, the things of the world have less attraction for us.

We tend to hold onto and find security in things we can see: money in the bank, good health, and strong relationships with those around us. But in reality, there is not enough money in the bank, a good enough health report, or good enough circumstances for anyone to be at peace in this world.

A fearful person acts as if they had just a little more money, a little better marriage, a little more secure job, all would be well, but this is a false reality. For the fearful person, things are never really well. True security is always just out of reach. Only when we understand that our only true security is found in Christ our Lord do we find true peace.

Thinking Biblically

In order to be an overcomer, we need to change the way we view our responsibility to God and our relationship with the world. To do this, we must allow the Holy Spirit to teach us to think biblically—that is, according to God's Word and God's ways. We must humble ourselves and receive His perspective on our lives.

We must think biblically or we will be overcome by everything around us. Clint Eastwood once starred in a movie entitled *Firefox*, in which he was to infiltrate the former Soviet Union and steal one of its high-tech planes so America could keep the balance of power intact.

In this movie, Clint had to learn to think in the Russian language because that was how the plane was programmed to react to the pilots. It was a great security tactic since few Americans could think according to a foreign language, let alone one as difficult as Russian.

Apply this to our own thought lives. In order to live according to the Spirit and live in our identities as overcomers, we need to learn how to think biblically, not according to our old patterns of fleshly thought. The Spirit does not think the same way as people in the world do.

In order to allow Him to control our thoughts and actions, we have to learn to think like Him. Then, like Clint Eastwood learning to think in Russian, the Holy Spirit will be free to pilot our lives soundly and not be competing with worldly thoughts.

It is amazing what the Spirit will reveal to you if you are open to receive from Him. I have been prepared in advance for good news and bad news, for encouraging circumstances and difficult circumstances. The Spirit will show you great and unsearchable things to help you in your life if you sincerely seek Him.

A Spiritual Battle

As you strive to be an overcomer, remember that your battle is not with individual sins, thoughts, or actions. It is a spiritual battle that goes much deeper.

> *"For though we walk in the flesh, we do not war after the flesh. For the weapons of our warfare are not carnal, but mighty through God to the pulling down of strongholds; Casting down imaginations, and every high thing that exalteth itself against the knowledge of God, and bringing into captivity every thought to the obedience of Christ" (2 Corinthians 10:3–5, kjv).*

This is the overcoming principle for all aspects of life. It all starts in our minds. If we can be victorious and think biblically at all times, God will allow us to approach life from His vantage point, and the overcoming life will naturally follow. We will overcome the world, the flesh, and Satan.

I have tested these principles in my own spiritual walk, and I can testify that God has been faithful. It does not mean that it has always been easy, but with God's grace and a strong commitment on your part, you can be faithful and keep His Word.

> *Do not conform any longer to the pattern of this world, but be transformed by the renewing of your mind. Then you will be able to test and approve what God's will is—his good, pleasing, and perfect will. (Romans 12:2)*

The benefits of our identity as an overcomer are more wonderful than we can imagine:

Overcomers are not tossed to and fro by life's circumstances, but take a stand in the arena of life and come out victorious, whether by life or by death. Either is acceptable, provided that God is glorified.

Overcomers are unstoppable. They can see what God has for them and they will accomplish it, no matter what. They are directed by God's love and Christ's perseverance.

Overcomers do not try to evaluate their own capacity in light of a situation but trust God for the proper way to deal with it. They know that the outcome will be the best possible given the circumstances.

If we have this kind of power as individuals, imagine what kind of power we have when we function together. When you allow God to work His will in you and other believers around you, there is a certain amount of suffering that will accompany that process. This also is part of who you are in Christ.

18

sufferers

So far, most of the attributes of our spiritual identity discussed in this book have been positive, but there are some very challenging attributes we need to discuss, as well. One of these is suffering.

We have been saying all along that we need to have a crucified life. This is not easy to do. Jesus said, if anyone would follow Him, he must take up his cross daily and follow Him (Luke 9:23). This is a hard way to live. It means continually turning away our fleshly wants and desires and following hard after the Spirit's call.

Jesus knows this part of the Christian life is challenging, but it is necessary if we are to make progress with our Lord. As with all spiritual things, the blessings are far greater than our momentary affliction.

In fact, there seems to be a correlation between sharing in Christ's sufferings and His glory. For example:

> *I consider that our present sufferings are not worth comparing with the glory that will be revealed in us (Romans 8:18).*

> *In bringing many sons to glory, it was fitting that God, for whom and through whom everything exists, should make the author of their salvation perfect through suffering. (Hebrews 2:10)*

There are many other verses that correlate our suffering with our future glory. Among them are Romans 8:17, 1 Peter 4:13, and 1 Peter 5:1.

Fellowship with Christ

The point is, there is a fellowship with Christ's sufferings that one must enter into in order to be intimate with the Lord. Without this fellowship, our relationship is not complete. Fortunately, we enter into this fellowship of suffering by choice.

In 2 Timothy 3:12, it says that if we live godly lives in Christ Jesus, we will be persecuted. If the world hated and persecuted Jesus, they will do the same to us. They did not need a reason to hate Him (John 15:25). Nor will they need a reason to hate us.

In Romans 8:36, the scriptures remind us that, "For your sake we face death all day long; we are considered as sheep to be slaughtered." In the surrounding verses, it is clear that we may suffer tribulation, distress, persecution, famine, nakedness, and the like.

Our promise is not that we will be spared these things, but that we will not be separated from the love of Christ while we endure them (see Chapter 25, "dearly loved").

Earlier in that same chapter, Paul writes, "I consider that our present sufferings are not worth comparing with the glory that will be revealed in us" (verse 18). Glory will be revealed in the saints one day, but we must be willing to endure hardship, suffering, and persecution until then.

Part of the reason that God allows us to suffer is to learn how to minister to and comfort others. If we, ourselves, have not suffered, how can we identify with and comfort others who are suffering?

Second Corinthians 1:3-7,kjv, gets to the core of this principle:

> *Blessed be the God and Father of our Lord Jesus Christ, the Father of mercies and God of all comfort, who comforteth us in all our tribulation, that we may be able to comfort them which are in any trouble, by the comfort wherewith we ourselves are comforted of God. For as the sufferings of Christ abound in us, so our consolation also aboundeth by Christ. And whether we be afflicted, it is for your consolation and salvation, which is effectual in the enduring of the same sufferings which we also suffer: or whether we be comforted, it is for your consolation and salvation. And our hope of you is steadfast, knowing, that as ye are partakers of the sufferings, so shall ye also be of the consolation.*

Another reason to suffer is to learn obedience. As our leader and example, Christ was made perfect in His obedience through suffering. In Hebrews 2:9,10 kjv, it declares,

> *"But we see Jesus, who was made a little lower than the angels for the suffering of death, crowned with glory and honor, that he by the grace of God should taste death for every man. For it became him, for whom are all things, and by whom are all things, in*

bringing many sons unto glory, to make the captain of their salvation perfect through sufferings."

This is explained a bit more in Hebrews 5:7-9,kjv:

"Who in the days of his flesh, when he had offered up prayers and supplications with strong crying and tears unto him that was able to save him from death, and was heard in that he feared; though he were a Son, yet learned he obedience by the things which he suffered; And being made perfect, he became the author of eternal salvation unto all them that obey him."

Building Perseverance and Hope

Thanks be to God that we do not suffer just for the sake of suffering, but that there is an eternal purpose. Sometimes that purpose is to strengthen and grow us in our faith.

Other times, it is to strengthen and encourage others. A Christian sister tells the story of a friend whose son was born with a crippling nerve disorder. When she met the man's son, the boy was 16 years old.

His speech, his ability to talk, and the position of his hands and arms, head, and legs were all severely affected by the disease. But despite these physical challenges, he was a happy, well-adjusted teenager.

When this woman first learned of the son's disease, her flesh immediately cried out, "What a terrible thing to happen to a man of God!" Then she learned something powerful. Of her friend's own immediate family (parents and siblings), he was the only one who had a personal relationship with Jesus. He had tried many times to share the gospel with them, but their hearts were hard. When his family discovered his son's disease, they had been horrified. But their shock quickly turned to amazement when, instead of being devastated or blaming God for their circumstances, he and his wife thanked God for their child.

They watched as they bore with grace and patience the trips to the hospital, the cost of the medical treatments, and the daily rituals of caring for their son. They watched as he and his wife glorified God every day for the blessing their son brought to their lives.

They were baffled. How could this couple have peace and joy? How could they be so happy and content? And yet, as the years passed, it became quite clear that this was no act. Despite their personal suffering, this was a joyful, loving family, full of the peace of the Lord.

Through this experience, her friend was able to share with his family the power of God in a very practical way that words could never do. And because her friend had taught his family the love and sovereignty of God, his son was not angry with God for his disease.

He loved the Lord. He had many wonderful Christian friends and was a blessing to everyone around him. Her friend said, "If this disease was necessary to reach the hearts of my family, then so be it."

That conversation humbled my Christian sister deeply and taught her an important lesson about the things of God.[4] When we understand that we suffer for a purpose and that all things work for good for those who love the Lord and are called according to His purpose (Romans 8:28), this helps us to persevere cheerfully and with genuine hope.

Part of the Package

Paul warned the believers around him that we could not enter the Kingdom of God without enduring many hardships. Congratulations! That is part of your spiritual identity package.

Peter leaves us with a good promise that we can claim as we go through difficulty. 1 Peter 5:10, kjv, declares,

> *"But the God of all grace, who hath called us unto his eternal glory by Christ Jesus, after that ye have suffered a while, make you perfect, stablish, strengthen, settle you."*

Earlier, he pointed out that God takes note if we suffer worthily. If we suffer for wrongdoing, that is not impressive, for that suffering is deserved. But when we suffer patiently when we are wronged, that gets God's attention—and His blessings (1 Peter 2:19).

There is no doubt that, as believers in Jesus, we will suffer. We must arm ourselves with the attitude of Christ and persevere through that suffering. We must use these experiences to gain glory for eternity, to minister comfort to others, and to allow suffering to perfect our obedience in the process. Then we will show ourselves to be true followers of our glorious Lord.

Earlier in this book, we discussed at length our privilege and challenge to overcome, but if the circumstances of our lives are always easy and smooth, what is there to overcome?

I believe this is why immigrants to America tend to have much more successful business track records than American-born individuals (I have heard an unsubstantiated 8:1 ratio of success in immigrants versus non-immigrants, which I tend to believe).

There is so much more to overcome— obstacles of language, education, culture, and employment— and the determination that enables immigrants to overcome these barriers also tends to catapult them to success.

An overlooked character quality that rises in importance when learning to overcome life's issues is servanthood.

19

servants

> *[Jesus speaking] Not so with you. Instead, whoever wants to become great among you must be your servant. For even the Son of Man did not come to be served, but to serve, and to give His life as a ransom for many.* (Mark 10:43, 45)

Our Main Example

Jesus came as a servant. He came to serve, to love, and to sacrifice His life for us. He did not come to dominate, control, or impose how we should live. Jesus was the greatest teacher of all time. He taught primarily by His own example. We would do well to follow that example.

At the end, He took off his outer garments, wrapped Himself in a towel, and washed His disciple's feet. He was clearly their Lord and yet His main lesson was servanthood (John 13:1-17).

He imparted to them that they should serve each other sacrificially when He was gone. His last demonstration of service was to freely die on the Cross. He willingly laid down His life for our salvation and to bring us closer to God.

No one can ever repay Jesus for being the servant that He was. No one can ever match what He accomplished. One thing we can do is to freely offer ourselves and be willing to become servants to emulate the Master's life.

In the Old Testament, there came a time where a slave could go free and debts would be forgiven. However, a slave could choose to remain a servant to his master. It required an awl to be driven into the person's earlobe against the doorpost. This ceremony sealed the fact that the servant permanently belonged to his master (Exodus 21:6).

God does not expect or ask us to perform that ceremony today, but to spiritually be given over to the Master as a servant is biblical New Testament Christianity. It takes a decision of the will and a commitment of the heart. Are you willing to be a servant of your Lord in this present age in which we live?

Throughout Jesus' life and ministry, He went about doing good and serving the needs of many people. I like to define ministry as "seeing and meeting needs." Pretty simple huh? If we make the decision to be His servant, we will also do much good for the Kingdom of God during our short tenures on the earth.

Qualities of a Servant

There are certain traits that accompany a servant of God. They must be learned because they are unnatural to us. The first trait is humility. You will find that a true servant of God is humble, like the Master. Jesus said of Himself that He was gentle and humble in heart

(Matthew 11:29). We need this humbleness of heart to serve properly.

A good example of this was Mother Theresa. One can know with certainty that this woman had humility and was not striving for position or honor for herself. No one can serve the dying and orphans in Calcutta the way she did with pride or selfishness as a driving force.

People with pride in their hearts want to be first and to have the control. People with pride have a motive of gain and self-benefit. They want to spend what they receive for themselves. This is not the way of a godly servant.

In 3 John 9-11, we see what happens when this servant pattern is not followed properly.

> *I wrote to the church, but Diotrephes, who loves to be first, will not welcome us. So when I come, I will call attention to what he is doing, spreading malicious nonsense about us. Not satisfied with that, he even refuses to welcome other believers. He also stops those who want to do so and puts them out of the church. Dear friend, do not imitate what is evil but what is good.*

Diotrephes was an elder and leader in the church, but he was lacking the humility of a servant. We see what the Apostle John's take was on this and to be sure, Jesus feels the same way.

The second trait of a servant is to be submissive. We know that we should submit to God (Proverbs 3:6, James 4:7), but the Word also imparts to us to submit to one another. Submit to one another out of reverence for Christ. (Ephesians 5:21)

In various places, it says to submit to others including earthly authorities (1 Peter 2:13, Romans 13:5), church leaders (Hebrews 13:17), husbands (Ephesians 5:22, 24), younger folks to elders (1 Peter 5:5), etc. To be able to submit is a servant's posture. A person who is unable to submit is disqualified from being a servant and will most likely suffer some form of punishment or discipline as a result.

I have learned that in trouble especially, it is wise to keep a submissive posture and to stay low to the ground, literally. On one occasion, I was attempting to reconcile two brothers who were at odds with each other over minor issues and negative perceptions.

As they sat in their chairs, I sank to the ground between them, appealing and cajoling them to drop their case against each other. My power was in my low position, my low posture. This is taking the low road of a servant. I believe that the Lord, in His grace, can more easily support and strengthen our cause, if we submit ourselves to Him and to one another.

A final trait of a servant is selflessness or "others-oriented." This requires a servant to be practical and observant. A seasoned waiter at a restaurant must notice when their patrons need water or anything of substance. A valuable employee will invest time and energy to help the business be profitable, no matter what the sacrifice.

Servant Leader

Thanks to the wisdom and management style of Robert Greenleaf, there was a surge in recent decades toward the concept of servant leadership. This concept espouses that the real leaders of any organization (business, church, non-profit) are servants who lead by their example and by their sacrifice for the good of all. Sound familiar? The idea comes from Jesus and is being incorporated, in part, into the fabric of our American lifestyle.

One example of a servant leader from our American history is George Washington. One rainy day during the American Revolutionary War, George Washington rode up to a group of soldiers attempting to raise a wooden beam to a high position. The corporal in charge was shouting encouragement, but the soldiers couldn't get the beam in position.

After watching their lack of success, Washington asked the corporal why he didn't join in and help, to which the corporal replied, "Don't you realize that I am the corporal?" Very politely, General Washington replied," I beg your pardon, Mr. Corporal, I did." Washington dismounted his horse and went to work with the soldiers to get the oak beam in position.

As they finished, General Washington was wiping perspiration from his face, and said: "If you should need help again, call on Washington, your commander-in-chief, and I will come."[5]

A servant does not seek his own agenda but considers God's interests and others ahead of himself. A positive example of this is found in Timothy as expressed by the Apostle Paul:

> *"I have no one else like him, who will show genuine concern for your welfare. For everyone looks out for their own interests, not those of Jesus Christ. But you know that Timothy has proved himself because as a son with his father he has served with me in the work of the gospel."* *(Philippians 2:20-22)*

Proof that Timothy loves the Lord is that he served with Paul in the work of the gospel. Timothy cared for the welfare of others and sought to meet the interests of Jesus Christ. Can we say that we do that? Do we have the desire?

One mark of a true servant is that they are a follower of Jesus. This is part of their spiritual identity, their spiritual DNA.

20

followers of Jesus

The Son of man must suffer many things, and be rejected of the elders and chief priests and scribes, and be slain, and be raised the third day. And [Jesus] said to them all, if any man will come after me, let him deny himself, and take up his cross daily, and follow me. For whosoever will save his life shall lose it: but whosoever will lose his life for my sake, the same shall save it. (Luke 9:22-24, kjv)

To Follow

The Kingdom of God is very different than the world. It operates on different principles. In the world, we speak much of leadership and the need for it. This is understandable. Even Jesus said the people were helpless and harassed, like sheep without a shepherd.

However, in the Kingdom, to lead, one must first learn to follow. In ancient Israel, there was a saying; to "follow in the dust of the rabbi." This meant that a man would commit himself for a time to actually follow in the footsteps of a rabbi who was training him. He would live life alongside the rabbi, observing his tone, his approach, his attitude, and his mannerisms in many life situations.

The modern-day expression of "follow in the dust of the rabbi" is "more is caught than taught." People learn more from example, hands-on experience, and on-the-job training than just an academic exercise with lots of information. To impart to another person implies that the student is open, teachable, humble, and willing to gain knowledge and experience from another. It is not that the classroom does not have its place, but to be mentored in an area of life, means getting out of the classroom and dealing with the messes and challenges of life.

Mentoring is an important principle these days in the business world and top firms know and understand the importance of their executives partaking in this type of program. The military also applies this same principle in their ranks to constantly encourage and stimulate growth and development of the individual, at whatever level they are. If there is a mentor, then there is a mentee who is learning and questioning and experimenting with the fundamentals of their work.

In the New Testament, we have Jesus as the Lord, setting an example for His followers. This individual follower is often called a disciple, which in the Greek means a learner, or a pupil, one who applies the discipline and rigors of His Master over time. In Luke 6:40 kjv it states, "The disciple is not above his master: but every one that is perfect shall be as his master."

This is the whole purpose of us as believers being committed followers of Jesus. It is one of our main spiritual identities and a lifelong process to be like Him through catching and emulating what we see in Him.

If we truly "follow in the dust of the Rabbi," we will gain His tone, His love, His mannerisms over time. This is not accomplished by simply reading the Bible as an academic exercise.

I like Joshua 1:8, kjv, as a key principle for the follower of Jesus.

> *"This book of the law shall not depart out of thy mouth; but thou shalt meditate therein day and night, that thou mayest observe to do according to all that is written therein: for then thou shalt make thy way prosperous, and then thou shalt have good success."*

This Word that Joshua is speaking of in the Old Testament has been expanded in the New Testament and is chock full of principles to live by and obey, so as to please God.

The New Testament has a similar passage in James 1:22-25:

> *"Do not merely listen to the word, and so deceive yourselves. Do what it says. Anyone who listens to the word but does not do what it says is like someone who looks at his face in a mirror and, after looking at himself, goes away and immediately forgets what he looks like. But whoever looks intently into the perfect law that gives freedom, and continues in it – not forgetting what they have heard, but doing it – they will be blessed in what they do.*

It says in John 1:14 that Jesus is the Word of God. It says this Word became life and we have seen His glory. This Word is both written and also spoken. In either case, Jesus is that Word and we would do well to hear it, listen to it, pay attention to it, meditate on it, submit to it, obey it, and teach it to others. As we do so, we are found to be transformed by it and blessed in it as we follow what the Lord requires of us.

Deny Yourself

I do not think you would get a debate among believers if you said that the main reason we follow Jesus is to become like Him. As Luke 9:22-24 says, if we would come after Him, we must deny ourselves. Sacrifice is at the heart of the gospel and what Jesus did for us by dying on the Cross. If we want to follow Him, we must follow His lead.

Romans 12:1-2 gives us a clue as to how we accomplish this.

> *"Therefore, I urge you, brothers and sisters, in view of God's mercy, to offer your bodies as a living sacrifice, holy and pleasing to God – this is your true and proper worship. Do not conform to the pattern of this world, but be transformed by the renewing of your mind. Then you will be able to test and approve what God's will is – his good, pleasing and perfect will.*

So, the passage says we must offer our bodies as a living sacrifice. Our daily commitment to sacrifice for His Kingdom will not physically kill us (as it would a real animal sacrifice), but it will kill certain worldly elements that are holding us back from being all the Lord wants us to be and to do. Our lusts and worldly ambition and anger and fleshly initiatives must be killed from within.

This is voluntary but takes very strong commitment on the disciple's part to allow it to happen, like a spiritual operation of sorts with the Spirit of God being the Chief Surgeon. Will you allow Him to operate, to deal with anything hindering the growth of the Kingdom within you?

If you do, then Romans 12:2 is activated and your mind will be renewed like a young child learning for the first time what life is all about. I call it hitting the reset button of understanding. When your mind is renewed, your life will be transformed in His Spirit from one degree to the next. 2 Corinthians 3:18, nlt, reveals this well-kept secret of how this transformation occurs:

> *"So all of us who have had that veil removed can see and reflect the glory of the Lord. And the Lord – who is the Spirit – makes us more and more like him as we are changed into his glorious image."*

Other translations make it clear that we are seeing this glory as in a mirror. As we look at ourselves, we are seeing Him instead. Somehow, as we are allowing ourselves to sacrifice for the Kingdom, the Lord changes us from the inside-out to appear more and more like Him.

For the follower of Jesus, this sacrifice must become a daily habit. Jesus says to pick up our cross daily. The idea is that God wants an expedient result. He wants us to be like Jesus as soon as is possible in the Spirit. This can be much quicker than any human effort seems possible.

But one thing is for sure, it can only happen if we are willing followers. Followers who are willing to sacrifice and to obey everything that the Lord is teaching us in His Word and in the world on a consistent and continuing basis.

And when we do obey everything, we can be sure that we will get resistance from the world and from its ruler.

21

Satan's adversaries

Lest Satan should get an advantage of us: for we are not ignorant of his devices. (2 Corinthians 2:11, kjv)

And it was given unto him to make war with the saints, and to overcome them: and power was given him over all kindreds, and tongues, and nations. (Revelation 13:7, kjv)

Competitive people will warn you never to underestimate an opponent. Satan is a formidable foe. He is an opponent who will take advantage of every weakness, every flaw, and every misunderstanding. Jesus said that when Satan lies, he speaks his native language, for he is a liar and the father of lies (John 8:44).

These are truths that are important for us to understand because every day, we are in the boxing ring with Satan. We are Satan's adversaries.

The scripture warns that Satan comes as an angel of light or a wolf in sheep's clothing. In other words, he is so subtle that we cannot judge by outward appearances; he will fool even the most discerning judge of earthly things.

In order to identify Satan, we must test the spirits (1 John 4:1) and apply wisdom and biblical principles to every situation.

Satan follows (or creates) the path of confusion and the slippery slopes of temptation, division, and pride. He roars like a lion to cause fear and paralyze. As believers, we have to test these things and not give in to his deceit.

I do not know about you, but I have heard of the most abusive incidents occurring between believers. One brother whom I know discovered that his pastor was sleeping with four or five of the women in the congregation.

He patiently dealt with the situation and finally was sued by the pastor for $80 million for slander (even though what he shared was true and he revealed the information only in the course of following biblical protocol). The pastor won the suit.

Fortunately, my friend had insurance to cover the loss. God worked some good through the situation by allowing my friend to be a witness to the unbelieving trial attorneys who fought hard for him. He kept his composure and suffered for the name, despite the fact that one believer is not supposed to bring another to court in front of unbelievers (1 Corinthians 6:1–8).

When these types of things occur, who do you think is behind them?

Rest assured, when a biblical principle is violated, Satan may be directly or indirectly involved. In order to defeat Satan, it is imperative that we do what Jesus did: We put on the whole spiritual armor of God.

What is our spiritual armor? We read about God's powerful battle dress in Ephesians 6:

> *Put on the whole armour of God, that ye may be able to stand against the wiles of the devil. For we wrestle not against flesh and blood, but against principalities, against powers, against the rulers of the darkness of this world, against spiritual wickedness in high places. Wherefore take unto you the whole armour of God, that you may be able to withstand in the evil day, and having done all, to stand. Stand therefore, having your loins girt about with truth, and having on the breastplate of righteousness; and your feet shod with the preparation of the gospel of peace; above all, taking the shield of faith, wherewith ye shall be able to quench all the fiery darts of the wicked. And take the helmet of salvation, and the sword of the spirit, which is the word of God: Praying always with all prayer and supplication in the Spirit, and watching thereunto with all perseverance and supplication for all saints. (Ephesians 6:11–18, kjv)*

What a powerful visual image! You will notice that we do not need great outward activity to defeat the devil and wickedness. We have only to take the right stand—a stand based on the Word, prayer, faithfulness, and faith.

Let's look at each of these elements more closely:

- *We stand in truth.* If we know what is true—based on the Word of God—when Satan whispers lies into your ears, you will recognize those lies as the falsehoods they really are.
- *We wear the breastplate of righteousness.* When we are secure in our identity in Christ (see Chapter 15, "holy and righteous"), it becomes much easier to gird ourselves in righteous behavior. But if Satan can find a crack in this armor, if he can get us to compromise our spiritual integrity, then it becomes easier to sin again, and again… and again. Wearing our breastplate of righteousness helps us to prevent Satan from getting a toehold into our hearts.
- *We stand in the gospel of peace.* God's command in the lives of believers is to make peace. As we have discussed, the spirit of enmity and discord have no place in God's kingdom. When we stand on the side of peace—on the side of unity among the brethren—we are living out biblical principles that allow the Holy Spirit to do His miraculous work.
- *Holding the shield of faith.* Our faith has more power than we can begin to imagine. It's been said that it's not how much faith we have, but in whom we place our faith that counts. When

we take our warfare into the realm of faith, we stop relying on our own limited strength, power, and wisdom and unleash the powers of the great I AM.

- *Donning the helmet of salvation.* The power of our armor starts with our relationship with God. Only those saved by the blood of the Lamb can claim the spiritual promises and power at God's disposal. It is the Helmet of Salvation that opens God's power to us.
- *The Sword of the Spirit.* The scripture says that the Word of God is "sharper than any two-edged sword, piercing between the bone and the marrow" (Hebrews 4:12). God's truth is contained in His Word, of which He said, "My words shall not return unto Me void, but shall accomplish what I please" (Isaiah 55:11, kjv). What a promise! When Jesus faced Satan in the wilderness, He fought back with only one weapon—the Word of God. It is no coincidence that in this weapon is contained all of the other weapons: truth, peace, righteousness, and faith.

Taking Your Stand

Embracing the truth about who you are in Christ is the first step in taking your stand against Satan. When we do, we know the outcome of the battle from the beginning.

The battle may be fierce, and Satan may bloody us along the way, but he does not win. The Word of God tells us that, for those who are blood-bought children of God, Satan is already a defeated foe (Romans 16:20).

Although he has been responsible for the blood of all the saints shed throughout history, God has given him a limited and temporary leash.

One day, justice will be served to him for his crimes:

> *And the devil, who deceived them, was thrown into the lake of burning sulfur, where the beast and the false prophet had been thrown. They will be tormented day and night for ever and ever. (Revelation 20:10)*

In the meantime, make no mistake. Satan is a powerful adversary. He will lie to you. He will try to trick you. He will do everything in his power to deceive you, tempt you into sin, and make you ineffective for God. If he cannot steal you from the Kingdom, then he will try to prevent anyone else from entering.

That means creating fear, causing doubt, and any other tactic he can to destroy your testimony or make you an ineffective witness. So take your enemy seriously.

I have clearly not overemphasized our adversary, the devil. But while I don't think the devil deserves credit, I don't want to ignore him, either. If allowed, Satan weasels his way into the brethren, into our families, and into our souls—but only if we let him. Do not let him.

Hopefully, you now have sufficient ammunition from this book to be the overcomer God called you to be. You now understand the practical outworking of the spiritual battle we are in against our enemy, the devil. When we take our stand against the enemy, we show ourselves to be ambassadors from another place.

22

ambassadors

We are therefore Christ's ambassadors, as though God were making his appeal through us. We implore you on Christ's behalf: Be reconciled to God. (2 Corinthians 5:20)

It is written, "Let the redeemed of the Lord say so." Why? Because if those Jesus has purchased with His own blood have nothing good to say about Him, then the rocks will cry out in praise. God desires a testimony, and He is asking us to be His living witnesses.

God's main assignment to every believer is to go into the world as His witness. Jesus' final exhortation before He ascended was,

> *"But ye shall receive power, after that the Holy Ghost is come upon you: and ye shall be witnesses unto me both in Jerusalem, and in all Judea, and in Samaria, and unto the uttermost part of the earth." (Acts 1:8, kjv)*

As God's ambassadors, we have to work our way outward. We start from where we are and press outward to wherever He wants us to be. To do this, we must be available to Him. The Lord will test us to see whether we are willing because He has no use for an unwilling servant.

Those of us who have every spiritual blessing in Christ (Ephesians 1:3) must be ready to give an answer for the hope that is in us (1 Peter 3:15) to anyone who asks. We should do it with grace, seasoned with salt (Colossians 4:5,6).

Paul gets down to the heart of the matter in 2 Corinthians 5 (v. 11,14,17–21) when he shares that we have both a ministry and a word of reconciliation. God is in the reconciliation business, and He wants us to be involved.

In this section of scripture, we find that both the terror and the love of Christ should constrain us to persuade people for His truth. It is here that God reveals that we act as though we were ambassadors for Christ as if God were making His appeal through us for others to be reconciled to God.

We know from our own lives the benefits of doing this, but it cannot be forced or imposed on others. In order for people to grasp it, they must hear, see, and understand this great news for themselves. This means seeing it, hearing it, and watching it lived out in us.

We are God's representatives to a lost world. Our behavior and how we carry ourselves reflect on the person we represent—God. So our actions are important, and more people are watching and scrutinizing us than we might think.

Many readers can attest to the fact that, over the years, they have found out that people were watching them, even when they did not know anyone was paying attention, or even that anyone was there at all.

Our actions can make a big difference, positively or negatively, in someone's perception of God. One famous evangelist once said that the world has yet to see what God can do through one man who was wholly yielded to Him.

An Old Testament scripture puts it this way: "The eyes of the Lord roam to and fro looking for those whose hearts are perfect toward Him" (2 Chronicles 16:9). God is looking for people to witness to the truth, people willing to sacrifice.

Living Martyrs

Most Christians are familiar with the term "martyr." Translated, it literally means, "witness." We normally think of a martyr as someone who lays down his or her life for the gospel, but God is also interested in living martyrs. Living martyrs are those who are willing to lay down their own needs, desires, and goals in order to accomplish His purposes, even at great personal cost.

Believe me, dear saint of the Most High God, this kind of sacrifice hurts. It is very difficult to lay down the things that are close to us in order to serve the things of God. By definition, sacrifice costs us something. What are you willing to give up in order to serve God?

Corrie Ten Boom was an example of a living martyr. Her family, providentially placed in German-occupied Holland during World War II was strategically hiding Jews to deliver them from the Nazis' persecution. The risk was great, but their sense of responsibility was greater.

This family made a great sacrifice. They were caught, and the whole family was split up and put into concentration camps. Corrie ended up with her sister, who grew ill and died in the camp.

But before she died, Corrie's sister ministered to and strengthened Corrie to enable her to represent the Lord, even in the midst of suffering.

By God's grace, Corrie rose to the occasion and was mightily used by God. She learned to be a living martyr, which may be even more difficult than being a martyr who goes to the death.

Either way, whether we live or die, we are committed to being witnesses for God. There are many believers today, especially in the Middle and Near East, who are killed for their faith.

There are also many believers who are sick in the body, but still lift up the name of the Lord and give Him glory. When we can praise the Lord's goodness, mercy, and love, even in the midst of suffering, there is no more powerful testimony!

Placed for Glory

God has strategically placed each of us to be His witnesses for the truth. If we remain open to Him, He can bring opportunities for us to be His ambassadors in every environment and circumstance.

In my early days as a believer, I was blessed to be trained by the Navigators, an evangelistic ministry headquartered in Colorado Springs. They taught me the biblical mandate and the need to share my faith with others.

Until then, I really thought that my faith was a private matter. In the summer of 1984, I was at Syracuse University, staying in one of the fraternities. One week's topic was focused on evangelism.

We went out with teams to give it a try. I was told to be myself and to share naturally what Jesus meant to me and to prayerfully approach these opportunities with love and grace. It was unforgettable. People were so open to me and I felt empowered by the Spirit to do this work, even though it was my first time. I have been trusting the Lord ever since to use me with the lost.

Not every follower of Jesus has the gift of evangelism, of course, but every believer is called to share the good news and to be ready to give a reason for the hope they have within them. God realizes that you have a certain personality and capacity.

He does not expect you to be someone you are not. He will use you right where you are if you commit to lovingly respond to the opportunities that He brings.

The following year, it became clear that I should trust the Lord to apply what I had learned from the Navigators in a more specific way. I asked the Lord to give me 20 souls who would trust Him for the first time.

I kept a journal, and sure enough, after the year was up, there were 20 people whom I had led to the saving knowledge of the Lord.

The next year, I asked for another 20 souls, and again, the Lord gave me exactly 20 who came to trust in Him. This time, however, I wrote a follow-up letter to each of them and found that many of their decisions for Christ did not hold very well, and they did not flourish in their early years of faith.

Sharing Your Life

Then God gave me a passage which changed my approach to evangelism:

> *"We were delighted to not only share the gospel of God with you, but our lives as well, because you had become so dear to us."* (1 Thessalonians 2:8)

Through this verse, God showed me that it is personal relationships—life on life—that changes lives for eternity. It's not just the one-time act of sharing the gospel, but a long-term discipleship that helps young converts go on and mature in their faith.

God has brought many people into my life to allow me the privilege of helping them grow. There have been many friends who have come and gone, and the results have been mixed. The reason is that the Parable of the Sower (Matthew 13:3–23) is still as relevant today as when Jesus first spoke it.

We are responsible for planting and watering, but the seeds fall on various types of soil. We cultivate, but God gives the increase (1 Corinthians 3:6).

God's desire is for people to open their hearts wide to Him. People must allow the ground to be broken up, tilled, and fertilized. The good news is that God promises that a crop—some thirty, some sixty, and some hundredfold—will come from a fertile heart.

Knock, Knock! It's Domino's

While involved with college ministry at Lehigh University, I was a Domino's pizza delivery boy. I spent most of the day in my car taking the pizza pies to hungry customers. As I prayed and earnestly sought the Lord, He allowed me to get fired up and share my faith as I drove around.

During this time, I saw formless faces, people without names. Who was this multitude? I wondered. Was I somehow connected to them? The answer, of course, was yes.

Several years later, after I graduated from college and ended up in the construction industry, I became involved with the Christian Business Men's Committee (CBMC).

They had a wonderful television program, based in Philadelphia, where men could share their faith on the air in the form of an interviewed testimony. I was interviewed and thought that it was a wonderful medium to share the good news. Later, I found out that the show was potentially going off the air because of a shortage of interviewees.

That same day, I was cutting through Philadelphia haphazardly and came to a red light. I looked up, and there was the TV station where the show was taped. Right then, God made it clear to me that He wanted me involved with the show. For four months, I recruited men to share on the program. Then, to my great surprise, I was asked to host the program.

For two years, I interviewed about one hundred men from all walks of life concerning their faith in Jesus and how relevant it was to their workplace. Approximately two million people watched those shows.

I realized that while driving for Domino's five years earlier, God had been preparing me to witness to millions of people I would never see.

Everyone has their own special gifts and is called by God to be a witness to the things which they have seen and heard. The Lord is faithful to bring us the opportunities He wants us involved in, whether sharing with our family and friends, co-workers, strangers, or people we will never meet.

Tilling With Prayer

Two final points I want to make concerning being an ambassador for the Lord. The first is that it is very important to be prayerful about such opportunities.

When I was with the Navigators, it was predetermined that, when we went out in pairs to share the gospel, one person's primary role was to pray during that time for the Lord to work, to prepare the hearts and the ears of the hearers.

We wanted to always be in prayer for sensitivity to such opportunities and not to shrink back when God brought them to us.

The second is that the Great Commission, recorded in Matthew 28:19–20, is the Lord's imperative. "Go into all the world and make disciples of all nations, baptizing them in the name of the Father, the Son, and the Holy Ghost, and teaching them to obey everything I have taught you." He gives us the authority from His Father to go and fulfill this commission.

Certainly, God has called each of us to be His witnesses, His ambassadors to live according to His command. My experience has been that great joy accompanies this task.

What a privilege it is to be His witness in a day when there are so many voices competing for a soul's attention! The more I have shared Christ over the years, however, the more I have noticed how my emphasis has changed. At first, the initial focus was on how well I presented.

Then it shifted to the content or message that I was sharing. Finally, it became clear that it was not the messenger or the message, but an emphasis on the person of God with sensitivity to the receiver.

The receiver, in turn, was checking out my life, as the messenger, to see if it matched my words. They wanted to know, could I be holy and righteous? Was there something attractive enough about me to make them take notice?

As children adopted into the family of Christ at salvation, we have been given a grave responsibility. Sometimes the Jesus in our lives is the only Jesus people see. If someone were never to hear of Jesus from anyone else, and you were the only example they would encounter, what kind of Jesus would they see? Or would they know they had encountered Jesus at all?

This is why, as part of our spiritual identity package, we have not only the privilege but the responsibility to be His ambassadors. But if we are outwardly ambassadors, what are we to be inward?

23

worshipers

Yet a time is coming and has now come when the true worshipers will worship the Father in the Spirit and in truth, for they are the kind of worshipers the Father seeks. (John 4:23)

The context of this verse is Jesus conversing with the woman at the well in Sychar, a foreign city for the Jews in Samaria. The disciples left Jesus alone as they went into town to buy food, and along came this woman to draw water from the well there.

It was against every custom, tradition, and religious law for Jesus to speak with her, but he did so anyway. He begins by asking for a drink and then launches the conversation, as only the Lord can, into spiritual things.

As the conversation went on, she argued that Samaria (including the mountain there because it was where Jacob, the Jewish patriarch had a history) was THE religious place to be. Jesus retorted by sharing that it is not the place that God is concerned with, but the people and the way in which they worship Him that matters.

This is what God is after; this is what He is seeking. This would have been quite a paradigm shift, not only for this Samaritan woman but for the Jews as well.

God is seeking worshipers, true worshipers. There are many religions in the world today. How many of them are worshiping the ONE true God, Creator of Heaven and Earth, the God of the Bible? The Bible says there is no one else like Him (in numerous verses).

One verse to illustrate the point is 2 Samuel 7:22 which says, "How great you are, Sovereign LORD! There is no one like you, and there is no God but you, as we have heard with our own ears."

False Gods and Idols

There are many false Gods, contrived Gods, and idols fashioned in people's hearts trying to replace God. But there is only one true God, the Maker of Heaven and Earth, who is sovereign, separate from time and space, and eternal. There is only one omniscient, one omnipotent, and one omnipresent God in the Universe and that is the God of the Bible.

Blaise Pascal, a French mathematician and philosopher, shared: "There is a God-shaped vacuum in the heart of every man which cannot be filled by any created thing, but only by God the Creator, made known through Jesus Christ." I believe this is true. I believe that people attempt to fill this vacuum with all sorts of things.

Whatever you try to fill this God-shaped vacuum with, it is by definition, an idol. Why? Because only God can fill that vacuum, that void. Things can never fill it up. As hard as we try and as much as we think we enjoy certain things, in the end, it becomes clear that we are chasing after the wind.

After Solomon tried almost everything that could be tried because of his wealth and stature, he realized it was all meaningless. His observation was, "I have seen all the things that are done under the sun; all of them are meaningless, a chasing after the wind (Ecclesiastes 1:14).

But when a person worships God, there is no wasted time or effort, because one cannot offer the praise, thanks, majesty, and glory that He is due. This is quite true. If all we did was constantly worship our God, it would not satisfy His worthiness.

The Bible says that He is a jealous God (Exodus 34:14). What is He jealous of? After all, He is God. He does not need anything, right?

Well, actually He desires our worship, our allegiance, our obedience. He sets up the Universe to be clear who He is, but faith is the needed ingredient to engage and approach Him. It is a mystery and a dichotomy. He desires to be close to us yet He lives in unapproachable light.

In addition, He decided not to make us robots to automatically love and obey Him, but free will agents to do as we choose. He is a spirit and He wants us to encounter Him in life and in a personal relationship. He will not force this on us, but He is definitely jealous for it.

Moses and God

Moses had some definite encounters with a jealous Jehovah God. As he was intrigued and attracted to God and His glory and majesty, he sought to see these attributes in close up fashion. Here's how the conversation ensued as the nation of Israel had just come out of Egypt:

> *Then Moses said, "Now show me your glory." And the LORD said, "I will cause all my goodness to pass in front of you, and I will proclaim my name, the LORD, in your presence. I will have mercy on whom I will have mercy, and I will have compassion on whom I will have compassion. But," he said, "you cannot see my face, for no one may see me and live." (Exodus 33:18-20)*

Moses was the one person who God really knew face to face and yet, even Moses could not get a front glimpse of the Eternal One. In the Old Testament, God was only knowable to a few to whom he revealed himself. He sent his Word through the prophets and gave instructions and commandments to the people for their good so God could have His blessing rest upon them.

There was a sense in which God kept His distance. He shared with Moses right before the aforementioned encounter that He would not go with Israel lest He destroy them on the way. God is Holy and He cannot tolerate evil or wrongdoing. It is against His very being.

Fast forward to the New Testament and we see a distant God drawing near through His Son. It is written,

> *"that at the name of Jesus every knee should bow, in heaven and on earth and under the earth, and every tongue acknowledge that Jesus Christ is Lord to the glory of God the Father." (Philippians 2:10-11)*

In the Old Testament, God allowed Israel to build a temple in Jerusalem so that the people could worship Him. There were very strict rules to be adhered to as God committed to dwelling in the Holy of Holies with His Shekinah Glory.

But, in the New Testament, we see that people have become God's temple (see chapter 14) and He dwells in their hearts by faith through the promised Holy Spirit.

Both Testaments

So whether it is the Old or the New Testaments, we see that God desires worship from a sincere people who worship in truth.

> *All nations whom thou hast made shall come and worship before thee, O Lord; and shall glorify Thy Name. (Psalm 86:9)*

God deserves our worship and the result is glory to Him. Often, we think we must be in a religious building to worship God, but it is clear that a person can worship God anywhere if it comes from the heart.

I like the picture of Jacob, that patriarch of the Jews. When he was about to draw his last breath, it says that he leaned on his staff, gathering all his remaining strength and worshiped God in the process. He spoke prophetic words to his children and their futures as he did so. What an awesome way to end life, to worship God and speak the future ahead of time as a legacy for your descendants' benefit.

When an individual worships God, they are being who they were created to be. When a person worships in the way of the spirit there is power, truth, and a witness that God himself is true.

The more we can see the awesomeness of our God, the more we will realize that we need to be daily worshipers of the One who brought us into existence and who has a wonderful plan for each of us, if we trust Him.

It is also clear as we read in Revelation that our future in eternity will be spent worshiping our God as a primary activity. If this is the case, isn't it wise to gain this worshiping posture while still on the earth?

If practice makes perfect, most of us, who are far from perfect in this realm of worship, obviously need a lot more practice. Not only that but since we do not see clearly who God really is, we do not comprehend the extent to which He deserves our whole life, our very all in all.

But he does deserve our whole life and as we give it to Him, we are blessed.

24

blessed

All these blessings will come on you and accompany you if you obey the LORD your God: You will be blessed in the city and blessed in the country. The fruit of your womb will be blessed, and the crops of your land and the young of your livestock – the calves of your herds and the lambs of your flocks. Your basket and your kneading trough will be blessed. You will be blessed when you come in and blessed when you go out. (Deuteronomy 28:3-6)

This Old Testament promise of blessing turned out to be true based on the history we observe. Whenever Israel turned away from sin and trusted the Lord, all went well for them. No one and nothing could touch them. During their days of obedience, they routed foreign nations, settled in the Promised Land, and were blessed in all they undertook.

One king was wise enough to know that it was going to take supernatural means and methods to overcome such a blessed people. He was Balak, king of Moab, and he was out to undermine and destroy Israel.

Three times he sought to curse Israel using Balaam the sorcerer, and three times God dealt with this unrighteous duo. Every time Balaam set out to curse Israel, he ended up blessing them instead. Balak was furious at the end of those attempts, but there was nothing he could do (Numbers 23:11).

I can say confidently, that as believers in Jesus, we are even more blessed than Israel of old. Jesus takes the blessings in Deuteronomy and applies them in New Testament fashion to again instill God's blessings as available to God's people. However, many of the reasons we are blessed are inward, spiritual reasons, not just outward and physical.

We are also now blessed for suffering and persecution, for being meek and merciful, for mourning and for spiritual desire to seek God (Matthew 5:3-12).

God appears to be blessing us more with His presence and His disposition and view of life, rather than just attainment of good things and special treatment. Can you see the difference from the Old Testament to the New Testament?

The Beatitudes

He said:

Blessed are the poor in spirit, for theirs is the kingdom of heaven.

Blessed are those who mourn, for they will be comforted.

Blessed are the meek, for they will inherit the earth.

Blessed are those who hunger and thirst for righteousness, for they will be filled.

Blessed are the merciful, for they will be shown mercy.

Blessed are the pure in heart, for they will see God.

Blessed are the peacemakers, for they will be called children of God.

Blessed are those who are persecuted because of righteousness, for theirs is the kingdom of heaven.

Blessed are you when people insult you, persecute you and falsely say all kinds of evil against you because of me. Rejoice and be glad, because great is your reward in heaven, for in the same way they persecuted the prophets who were before you. (Matthew 5:3-12)

Jesus is clear in the Beatitudes that we are blessed in so many ways. The blessings are not just outward and material, but as I shared, they are inward and spiritual, and not dependent on circumstances, events, or time.

It means that bad things can be happening to you, but you are still blessed regardless. Of course, it is understood that you are not sowing bad or evil behavior, but good and upright actions.

For example, Jesus was blessed by His heavenly father, yet He suffered and died a criminal's death, despite His innocence. If we follow the Master as His disciples, we should expect difficulties, trials, and suffering. Are we any better than Jesus? No, we are not. But, if He suffered being perfect, how much more will we suffer, being imperfect?

There is also a distinction in the New Testament that I see that transcends time and space. What I mean is that our blessings in Jesus are not restricted to just this time on the earth.

There are eternal implications to our blessed status now and it goes exponentially further than the Old Covenant blessings did. I see that our blessed lives can also impact heaven and other parts of the world like never before.

Our actions as individuals and part of His Body seem to have far-reaching ramifications according to what I read in the Bible. God has included us as part of His plan to impact the world for good.

Every Spiritual Blessing

Realize also that Jesus was blessed, and so are we, as believers, in this world. We are linked and joined to Him eternally. Samples of the many benefits we have are outlined in Ephesians chapter 1, but I consider verse 3 to be a key summary thought for the entire chapter.

> *Praise be to the God and Father of our Lord Jesus Christ, who has blessed us in the heavenly realms with every spiritual blessing in Christ. (Ephesians 1:3)*

Wow. We have been, past tense, blessed with every spiritual blessing in Christ (read through the chapter to see everything we have been blessed with). It is overwhelming.

Ephesians also paints a picture of us, as His believers, seated with him far above in the heavenly realms (2:6). Of course, many of us are unaware of our high position, which is a shame.

Every blessing really originates with God and is spiritual in nature. With God, the spiritual comes first, because He is spirit (John 4:24).

Any blessing we receive in this life originates with God and in the Spirit. Everything we receive is for our enjoyment and to give praise and thanks to the One who loved us and won't withhold any good thing from us. God is the most generous parent, without peer.

Please realize, dear believer that the best and truest blessings come from the Spirit. God is in the business of constituting us with his Son. If He can accomplish that in us, there is no blessing that we cannot experience in this world and the one to come.

Final Blessing

The biggest blessing we have is being in God's presence (Psalm 16:11) for eternity, beginning now. If we can fathom the depth and the riches of God, then we can begin to understand the awesomeness of His person. It is because of Him that we are blessed, but that realization can carry us through all of this life and beyond.

And in that blessing, we will realize that we are very much loved.

25

dearly loved

Therefore, as God's chosen people, holy and dearly loved… (Colossians 3:12)

The Bible is clear that believers are dearly loved by God. This is a foundational truth that all Christians need to receive for their spiritual well-being.

Love is a preeminent topic in God's Word and has application to each of our daily lives. As Christians, we are to excel in love toward God and man, but first, we must understand the truth that God loves us. Everything else flows from that.

Let's test your knowledge with a little Bible trivia quiz. What chapter in the New Testament speaks the most strongly about love? Did you say 1 Corinthians 13? Good guess, but I want to show you a chapter that has nearly double the references to love as that one. Ready? It's 1 John, Chapter 4. This is really the love chapter.

Let me run through some truths in 1 John 4 so you can see what the Word says about God's love toward us.

Love comes from God. (v. 7)

God is love. (v. 8)

This is how God showed His love among us: He sent His one and only Son into the world that we might live through Him. (v. 9)

Not that we loved God, but that He loved us. (v. 10)

Since God so loved us, we also ought to love one another. (v. 11)

If we love one another, God lives in us and His love is made complete in us. (v. 12)

And so we know and rely on the love God has for us. God is love. Whoever lives in love lives in God, and God in him. (v. 16)

We love because He first loved us. (v. 19)

This chapter continues to expand on the many facets of love and clearly shows that we can only love because of God. His loving initiative toward us opened the door for us to love also. We can only love—truly love—because He loved us first.

The Greatest Love

We know from Jesus that "Greater love has no one than this, that he lay down his life for his friends" (John 15:13). Jesus demonstrated this great love by His willingness to lay down His life at Calvary for you and me. God didn't wait for mankind to get it together before He suffered and died to save us from our sins.

He made this sacrifice while man was in the depth of his depravity. "But God demonstrates his own love for us in this: While we were still sinners, Christ died for us" (Romans 5:8).

In Romans 8:32, it also says, "He who did not spare his own Son, but gave him up for us all—how will he not also, along with him, graciously give us all things?"

The heart of love is sacrifice and a giving spirit. God is the originator of love and Jesus is His personal example.

Tap Into the Love Dispenser

Now, it is of the utmost importance that every believer in Jesus personally receives God's love on a continuing basis. One of the chief methods by which we do this is through the Holy Spirit. "[B]ecause the love of God is shed abroad in our hearts by the Holy Ghost, which is given unto us" (Romans 5:5, kjv).

In order to receive that love, we must make sure that the Spirit has full rule and reign in our hearts and is allowed to express His love in whatever way He deems fit for the situation.

How do you do this? First, you do this through your obedience. Sin clouds the communication lines to God. Think of it as like having static on your phone line. The more static you have, the harder it is to hear the person on the other end. Likewise, the more sin you have in your life, the harder it is to hear the Holy Spirit and to experience His love.

Second, you do this by simply asking. Jesus said, "For everyone who asks receives" (Matthew 7:8). God wants to deepen His relationship with you, so this is one prayer He loves to answer! While He knows your prayers before you even speak them (Isaiah 65:24; Matthew 6:8), He loves to hear you ask.

So pray continually that you would receive God's love in the fullest sense and seek to be filled with the Holy

Spirit. Finally, be ready to pour that love back out to others around you. Often, believers don't sense the love of the Holy Spirit because they don't open themselves to the Spirit's loving influence and control (read Romans 8:9).

Try this: Wherever you are, whatever you are doing, ask God to help you release His love. Just proclaim, "Lord, I release your love through the Spirit, the love you had at Calvary." You will be astounded as God releases His love in your situation.

Do You Really Believe?

Unfortunately, there is a sickness whose symptoms manifest themselves in the Church. It has always been this way. There appear to be believers who do not believe that God loves them.

Oh, they say the right things and have fine-sounding words, but wisdom is proven by actions. A lack of understanding and experience with God's unconditional love is the root of the problem.

If an individual really and truly believes that God loves them, he or she will naturally respond in gratitude for that love by obedience. Therefore, believers who truly embrace God's love also follow His Word. If you do not follow His commands, not only are you not loving God, but you are likely not receiving God's love for you, either. You are fooling yourself.

Jesus put it this way:

> *"Whoever has my commands and obeys them, he is the one who loves me. He who loves me will be*

loved by my father, and I, too, will love him and show myself to him" (John 14:21) It is implied that if you do not obey God's commands, you do not love Jesus.

There is an indirect warning in this passage, too. "[H]e who loves me will be loved by my father, and I, too, will love him and show myself to him" (emphasis mine). There is a direct relationship between obeying God through His Word and the amount of spiritual insight you receive from God.

His desire is to give you all you need for life and godliness (2 Peter 1:3), but He will not force the issue. If you are not obeying His Word, you close off the path to truth that God desires to show you (Jeremiah 33:3).

As believers, we must prove to be faithful to God by hearing and doing what His Word says to do. Only then can we receive the full measure of God's love.

It is not enough to see or know what God wants us to do. Our true spiritual identity is confirmed when we do what God expects us to do.

Obedience is difficult. To stay on course and not waiver, we must have faith that God's Word is true and that it is for our encouragement and edification (2 Peter 1:19–21, Romans 15:4). As the Word says, "let God be true and every man a liar" (Romans 3:4).

The longer we are alive, the more we should understand that God is true and that people falter in many ways. Even the best person cannot be trusted all the time in their words and deeds.

Oh, how we need God's love to cover us and keep us from evil! Jesus warned us, "The Spirit gives life; the flesh counts for nothing" (John 6:63). If God's love is to make a difference in who and what we are, we must learn the difference between the flesh and the spirit so that we can choose the spirit on every occasion and receive God's love at all times.

The next and last chapter will summarize what we have learned so that you can behave based on a rock-solid belief in your true spiritual identity.

26

CONCLUSION: behave as you believe

As a man thinks in his heart, so is he. (Proverbs 23:7, kjv)

Hopefully, dear reader, you have been stimulated and encouraged in your faith to realize what the Bible says about you as a believer in Jesus.

The New Testament has glorious things to say about us. These things are so wonderful, so staggering in their implications, that they are almost difficult to believe.

I admit that there are times when my spiritual identity has seemed too good to be true and my flesh has wanted to believe that the old man is resident and in control. Those voices are still faintly heard, but thanks be to God, the Spirit has trained me (and hopefully you) to believe the truth about who Christ is in me and who I am in Him and to shun voices that whisper to the contrary.

Spiritual Stakes

These foundational truths have acted as spiritual stakes that allow me to go higher and further in my walk with the King of kings. In fact, I dare say that I have never seen anyone go on with the Lord to maturity without realizing, to a large extent, the reality of their spiritual identity.

Sometimes, when you go to the park, there is a sketch artist sitting under a tree, offering to draw portraits of anyone who passes by. Participants sit down and wait patiently as the artist sketches their outline, one stroke at a time.

At first, the portrait doesn't look like much, but over time, as more strokes are added, the image begins to take shape. By the time the artist is finished, the likeness to the individual is amazing.

I hope that the chapters in this book have acted much like the strokes of an artist's pen. In each chapter, I have attempted to outline one characteristic in our spiritual identity, so by the time you reached the end of the book, the picture would be full.

In a nutshell, what does this identity look like?

- We are not the Creator, but the creation. We only find our true identities when we submit to His Sovereign will.
- We are God's children. We are sons and daughters and part of his spiritual family.
- We are heirs with Christ. We have an inheritance waiting for us to enjoy for eternity.
- We are kings in His kingdom. We rule, reign, and judge the things of the kingdom. He has given us unimaginable responsibility.

- We are God's friends. We are His children, with whom He desires to fellowship on a daily basis. He wants to talk with us, walk with us, and just hang out with us.
- We are masterpieces, created in Christ to perform good works. We are God's poem, his work of art and his proud achievement through His Son.
- We are new creatures. Once we give our hearts to Christ, the old person has passed away. Everything about our lives is fresh and new.
- We are Spiritual beings. Sin and the flesh no longer have power over us. When we walk in this identity, allowing our lives to be directed and controlled by the Spirit, the power of sin and the flesh is broken.
- We are ministers. We not only serve God but those around us. We are God's "go to" people—His hands for serving the deepest, most critical needs around us.
- We are priests to God. We live to serve Him through our praise, worship, and obedience. We no longer live for ourselves, but for Him.
- We are members of One body. Neither can we function wholly independent of the Body, nor can the Body function wholly independent of us.

- We are temples of God. He lives within us, guiding, directing, inspiring, and convicting us every moment of every day.
- We are holy and righteous. We may not feel holy and righteous, but with the Spirit living in us, that's how God sees us.
- We are saints of God. When God looks at us, He does not see us as sinners. He sees believers redeemed to Him by the blood of the Lamb.
- We are overcomers. We are given power, responsibility, and authority, and we can use these gifts and tools to accomplish any task that God gives us.
- We are sufferers with Christ. This allows us to identify more closely with our Savior and allow the miracle of God's power, strength, and glory to become reality for us.
- We are servants. We follow Jesus' example and lead by being the least of all.
- We are followers of Jesus. We follow in the dust of the Rabbi and learn all we can by being His disciples.
- We are Satan's adversaries. We are the front-line defense in a spiritual battle with the highest stakes. God has trusted us with His most precious possessions—the souls of those around us—and it is our job to fight for them with every weapon at our disposal.

- We are God's ambassadors to a lost and dying world. He isn't sending someone else to share His truth. He is sending us.
- We are worshipers of God. We worship in spirit and in truth. We display a lifestyle of worship and offer praise and our very lives on the altar of God.
- We are blessed because of God, his salvation and in His continual presence. No matter where we go or what we do we experience God's favor and blessing.
- We are dearly loved. We cannot even begin to fathom the depth and breadth of God's love for us.

What a portrait! When you see it all together, it's nearly impossible to comprehend. And yet, it's true.

New Perception, New Thinking

Of course, just because something is true doesn't mean that we believe it. Nor does it mean that we are appropriating this truth and making it effective in our lives.

I have seen older believers who are still infants in their spiritual walks because they have not yet understood their spiritual identity. Consequently, they have been unproductive and ineffective for the Kingdom of God. Certainly, we do not want to be numbered with this group!

Hopefully, your thinking has been challenged to grab hold of this amazing truth. Through faith, you have a new spiritual identity. You are seated with Christ in the heavenlies (Ephesians 2:6) and every spiritual blessing is yours (Ephesians 1:3).

You will reign on the earth one day, judging the world and angels. This is not always the easiest identity to live up to. In our new identities, we gain a new adversary. Satan will do everything he can to cause us to question our spiritual identity and cause us to stumble.

But God's grace is greater, and it is when the going gets tough, then His grace truly kicks into the highest gear. The more difficult it becomes, the more God's grace is there to help us through it.

How Much Are You Faithful With?

There is a powerful scriptural principle on which I would like to conclude. To the extent that you have been faithful with little, the Lord will entrust you with much (Luke 19:17). Our time is short, and we must grab hold of these truths now. We need to apply our spiritual identity in every circumstance of every day, showing ourselves to be the overcomers that the Lord calls us to be. The more we prove ourselves trustworthy with the things of God, the more He will trust us with in the future. What a privilege! He has given you everything you need to succeed.

My prayer is that you will know who you are in the Lord—a saint of the Most High God, who is holy, righteous, a witness to His glory, a fellow sufferer with Christ, a friend who is dearly loved and who walks according to the Spirit and not the flesh, a brother or sister who desires to be one with those in the local congregation in which the Lord has placed them, one who is God's temple, in whom God's spirit dwells by faith, and who has practiced overcoming everything that presents itself.

You understand that you are a new creature in Him and made to be a priest and king before our God, an able minister of the New Testament.

All these things are for us and for our help so that our joy may be complete in our Good Shepherd. All God's promises are "yes" and "amen," for us who are the first fruits of His grace during these powerful times. As children of God, rest assured that you will gain the promised inheritance if you stand firm in your faith until the end.

Spiritual Identity Vision and Application

Being trained and exposed to the Navigator Ministries over the years has been invaluable to me. One very important lesson I learned is the need to apply in my life what God is teaching me while it is still fresh. Now, I encourage you to do the same. Ask yourself the following questions:

What can I do now, armed with a fresh vision of my spiritual identity, to make a difference in my work, ministry, education, devotion, and relationships?

How should each of the 24 aspects of my spiritual identity change my thinking and my actions as I strive to be who God is calling me to be?

What areas of my biblical understanding need to be strengthened in the coming days to bolster my faith and my approach to life?

Is there one truth that God overwhelmingly impressed upon my heart from this book? What is my basic plan of action?

A Final Encouragement

I pray for everyone who reads this book to faithfully apply it, to cry out in commitment to the God of our salvation, and to share these truths with fellow brothers or sisters who see themselves after the flesh instead of the New Testament pattern.

The world has yet to see what God can do through one person who is wholly committed to Him. Will you take a stand and be that person for your Lord where you live and work? God will bless and multiply you and your ministry exponentially to His glory. Amen.

Index of biblical references by chapter

Dedication
Galatians 2:20
Introduction
Ecclesiastes 12:12
1 Corinthians 15:50–54
Chapter 1 — Mirror, Mirror on the Wall
John 1:12
1 John 5:11–13
Revelation 1:10,11, kjv
James 1:23,24, kjv
2 Corinthians 3:17,18, kjv
Chapter 2 — Who You Are Not
Job 38:4–13, 16–21
Job 40:5
Job 38-41
1 Corinthians 2:14
Joshua 5:13–15
John 6:45
Ephesians 2:1–3, kjv
Isaiah 64:6
Genesis 6:5–7
Chapter 3 - Children of God
1 John 3:1-2
John 1:12
Romans 8:16
Romans 8:15
James 1:17
Hebrews 13:8
Ephesians 1:6, kjv
Hebrews 13:5
Psalm 62:8
John 5:24
Matthew 6:33
Psalm 37:4, nasb
Ephesians 3:20
Revelation 17:14, 19:16
1 John 3:2
Jeremiah 29:11
Chapter 4 - Heirs
Romans 8:17
Titus 3:7, kjv
Ephesians 1:14, 18
Colossians 3:24
Hebrews 9:15
1 Peter 1:4, kjv

1 Peter 3:7
Chapter 5 – Kings
Revelation 5: 9,10, kjv
1 Corinthians 4:8
2 Timothy 2:12
Revelation 5:10
Revelation 20:6
Revelation 22:5
1 Corinthians 6:2,3
Matthew 28:18–20, nkjv
Hebrews 13:5
Colossians 3:4
Proverbs 20:1
Matthew 5:16
Acts 24:16
Chapter 6 – God's Friends
John 15:13–15, kjv
Matthew 24:12
1 John 4:20
James 4:8
Matthew 7:6, kjv
Hebrews 6:6, kjv
Proverbs 20:6
Isaiah. 66:1,2
Luke 6:30
Chapter 7 – Masterpieces
Ephesians 2:10, nlt
Romans 1:20
Colossians 2:10, kjv
Ecclesiastes 4:9-12
John 1:12
Philippians 2:16
Ephesians 2:10, nlt
Chapter 8 – New Creatures
2 Corinthians 5:17, kjv
Ephesians 4:24
John 1:12,13
Titus 3:5, kjv
Acts 4:20
Acts 4:12
1 Corinthians 15:22, kjv
Hebrews 2:10, kjv
Acts 3:15
John 18:6
Isaiah 9:6
John 16:33
Isaiah 9:6
Ephesians 2:10
1 Peter 2:11
Philippians 2:15
Matthew 6:25–33
Romans 8:28
John 1:12
Galatians 3:26
1 John 3:10

Romans 9:8
Chapter 9 - Spiritual Beings Part One
John 4:23-24
2 Corinthians 4:16
John 6:63
Jeremiah 15:16
John 3:1-21
Joshua 1:8
John 14:16-17
Ephesians 1:13-14
Luke 20:37-38
Chapter 10—Spiritual Beings Part Two
John 6:63
2 Corinthians 5:1
Galatians 5:19–21, kjv
1 Corinthians 15:31
Galatians 5:16–26, kjv
Luke 16:10
Song of Solomon 2:15
Proverbs 19:11
John 6:63, kjv
Romans 6:6–11
Romans 5:20
2 Corinthians 5:17
Romans 6:11
Romans 6:19
John 15
Philippians 2:12
2 Corinthians 9:8
Philippians 1:6
Ephesians 1:13,14
Chapter 11 — Ministers
2 Corinthians 3:5,6, kjv
2 Samuel 23:10
Zechariah 9:12
Matthew 11:30
1 Corinthians 12:4–6, nkjv
Ephesians 3:10
Romans 9:16
2 Corinthians 12: 9,10
Hebrews 4:9–11
2 Corinthians 12:9, nkjv
Chapter 12 — priests
Revelation 1:5,6, 5:9,10, nkjv
1 Peter 2:5, nkjv
1 Peter 2:9, nkjv
Hebrews 13:15
Psalm 51:17
Isaiah 66:2
Isaiah 66:3, nkjv
Psalm 90:12
Ephesians 5:16, kjv
Revelation 5:8, 8:3,4
Hebrews 4:16

John 16:24
1 Timothy 2:5
Hebrews 4:14
Hebrews 10:20
Hebrews 7:23–28
Hebrews 10:12
Hebrews 10:19–22
Hebrews 7:16
Hebrews 7:25, kjv
Chapter 13 — members of one body
Ephesians 3:10
John 17:20–23
Ezekiel 1:16–21
Genesis 11:6
Amos 3:3
Jude 8-10
1 Corinthians 1:10
1 Peter 5
John 17:20-23
John 5:19
John 8:28
Luke 4:14
1 Timothy 3:16, kjv
Philippians 2:6, kjv
John 13:35
Chapter 14 — temples
1 Corinthians 6:19,20
Ephesians 2:10
Romans 10:4
John 6:58
John 10:11
Matthew 28:18
John 4:20–24
Psalm 90:1
John 15:5
John 14:23,26
Acts 19:2–7
Acts 5:1–11
Matthew 5:13
1 John 5:16
2 Corinthians 13:5,6, j.b. phillips
2 Corinthians 6:16 j.b. phillips
1 Corinthians 6:19,20
Chapter 15 — holy and righteous
Rom. 5:19
Ephesians 1:4
2 Peter 1:3,4
Ecclesiastes 3:11
2 Corinthians 5:21
1 John 3:7, kjv
1 Peter 2:11
Philippians 2:12,13
Chapter 16 — saints
1 John 1:10

1 Peter 4:17,18
Psalm 1:5
Psalm 26:9
Psalm 51:13
1 John 3:9,10, kjv
John 16:13
1 Corinthians 2:12–16
1 Corinthians 2:16
1 John 3
Matthew 12:35
Luke 6:45
Philippians 4:8
Matthew 25:46, kjv
Romans 5:19
Luke 5:32
John 9:31
John 16:24
Romans 5:8
Hebrews 12
Jeremiah 29:11
1 Timothy 1:15
James 4:8
1 Corinthians 3:11–13
Psalm 103:12
1 Thessalonians 3:13, kjv
Ephesians 1:1
Chapter 17 — overcomers!
Revelation 12:11
John 16:33
1 John 2:15–17
Psalm 37:4
Matthew 6:18–33
1 John 5:4,5
Romans 8:26
1 Corinthians 10:13
2 Corinthians 12:9
Romans 6:6,12, kjv
1 John 2:13,14
Matthew 4
2 Corinthians 10:3–5
James 4:7,10
1 John 4:18
Jeremiah 29:11
Romans 8:1
2 Corinthians 10:3–5, kjv
Romans 12:2
Chapter 18 — sufferers
Luke 9:23
Romans 8:18
Hebrews 2:10
Romans 8:17
1 Peter 4:13
1 Peter 5:1
2 Timothy 3:12
John 15:25

Romans 8:36
Romans 8:18
2 Corinthians 1:3–7, kjv
Hebrews 2:9,10, kjv
Hebrews 5:7–9, kjv
Romans 8:28
1 Peter 5:10, kjv
1 Peter 2:19
Chapter 19 - servants
Mark 10:43, 45
John 13:1-17
Exodus 21:6
Matthew 11:29
3 John 9-11
Proverbs 3:6, James 4:7
Ephesians 5:21
1 Peter 2:13, Romans 13:5
Hebrews 13:17
Ephesians 5:22, 24
1 Peter 5:5
Philippians 2:20-22
Chapter 20 - followers of Jesus
Luke 9:22-24 KJV
Luke 6:40
Joshua 1:8 KJV
James 1:22-25
John 1:14
Luke 9:22-24
Romans 12:1-2
2 Corinthians 3:18 NLT
Chapter 21 — Satan's adversaries
2 Corinthians 2:11, kjv
Revelation 13:7, kjv
John 8:44
1 John 4:1
1 Corinthians 6:1–8
Ephesians 6:11–18, kjv
Hebrews 4:12
Isaiah 55:11, kjv
Romans 16:20
Revelation 20:10
Chapter 22 — ambassadors
2 Corinthians 5:20
Psalm 107:2, kjv
Acts 1:8, kjv
Ephesians 1:3
1 Peter 3:15
Colossians 4:5,6
2 Corinthians 5:11,14,17–21
2 Chronicles 16:9
1 Thessalonians 2:8
Matthew 13:3–23
1 Corinthians 3:6

Matthew 28:19,20
Chapter 23 – worshipers
John 4:23
2 Samuel 7:22
Ecclesiastes 1:14
Exodus 34:14
Exodus 33:18-20
Philippians 2:10-11
Psalm 86:9
Chapter 24 – blessed
Deuteronomy 28:3-6
Numbers 23:11
Matthew 5:3-12
Ephesians 1:3
Ephesians 2:6
John 4:24
Psalm 16:11
Chapter 25 — dearly loved
Colossians 3:12
1 John 4:7–12,16,19
John 15:13
Romans 5:8
Romans 8:32
Romans 5:5, kjv
Matthew 7:8
Isaiah 65:24
Matthew 6:8
Romans 8:9
John 14:21
2 Peter 1:3
Jeremiah 33:3
James 1:22–24, kjv
2 Peter 1:19–21
Romans 15:4
Romans 3:4
John 6:63
Chapter 26 — conclusion: behave as you believe
Proverbs 23:7, kjv
Ephesians 2:6
Ephesians 1:3
Luke 19:17

Endnotes

1 Pilgrim's Progress, L. Edward Hazelbaker, Bridge-Logos: Gainesville, FL, 1998, pp. 378–379.

2 Beware of the niv's translation of the word flesh (sarx in the Greek) as "sinful nature." It is misleading. A good resource to help you think through this is Birthright by David Needham. He does a thorough job expositing Romans 5–8, explaining pertinent terms why the flesh and the sinful nature are not the same. He emphatically expresses how our nature as believers is to not sin anymore. Needham's position contradicts a popular view—that we are all sinners. He describes and provides evidence to support that, as born-again believers, we are not sinners, but "saints."

3 Chapter 13 – Tower of Babel
https://en.wikipedia.org/wiki/Tower_of_Babel

4 Story reprinted, with permission, from Before God's Wrath, H. L. Nigro, Bellefonte, PA: Strong Tower Publishing, 2004, p. 232.

5 http://stephenblandino.com/2012/01/george-washington-on-servant-leadership.html

Word Search Puzzle

G	O	D	S	F	R	I	E	N	D	S	Q	B	T	K	S	I	J	O	U
A	S	E	I	R	A	S	R	E	V	D	A	S	N	A	T	A	S	W	P
B	A	Y	U	R	E	N	E	W	C	R	E	A	T	U	R	E	S	H	S
S	E	S	I	T	S	R	Q	S	N	P	R	I	E	S	T	S	S	O	L
S	N	H	A	E	G	R	E	G	U	Y	S	E	U	C	T	L	G	Y	L
A	Y	F	A	T	S	R	H	F	E	J	E	M	Q	N	K	B	N	O	A
S	E	G	K	V	R	B	I	N	F	N	N	C	I	N	L	C	I	U	W
E	H	P	O	M	E	C	Q	F	W	U	O	A	Y	A	C	E	E	A	E
C	Y	W	B	A	T	F	K	P	Y	V	S	T	G	F	C	M	B	R	H
E	D	S	C	T	S	G	O	C	E	R	U	C	I	S	H	Z	L	E	T
I	O	U	R	L	I	T	V	R	D	S	O	S	G	N	I	K	A	N	N
P	B	S	Z	S	N	P	C	S	I	E	E	I	D	Y	L	P	U	O	O
R	E	E	W	R	I	O	X	E	M	L	T	R	E	J	D	O	T	T	R
E	N	J	E	I	M	T	R	A	D	P	H	O	V	K	R	X	I	G	O
T	O	F	N	E	I	I	F	C	I	M	G	E	O	A	E	P	R	O	R
S	F	O	R	H	N	O	N	J	G	E	I	B	L	M	N	Y	I	D	R
A	O	S	B	Q	I	K	N	U	F	T	R	S	Y	B	O	T	P	T	I
M	S	R	A	D	S	N	D	I	E	R	D	C	L	A	F	Y	S	C	M
D	R	E	V	A	R	T	A	W	L	Y	N	B	R	S	G	A	M	F	R
E	E	W	B	C	E	Y	K	J	E	O	A	V	A	S	O	I	E	B	O
S	B	O	F	J	U	C	L	R	N	N	Y	S	E	A	D	Q	J	U	R
S	M	L	X	Z	F	I	M	S	I	T	L	U	D	D	M	I	K	A	R
E	E	L	D	D	E	I	R	F	S	D	O	G	L	O	S	X	L	B	I
L	M	O	U	S	A	M	F	A	C	N	H	A	T	R	E	F	A	U	M
B	I	F	K	Q	W	O	R	S	H	I	P	E	R	S	J	R	Q	B	X

AMBASSADORS
BEHAVE
BLESSED
CHILDREN OF GOD
DEARLY LOVED
FOLLOWERS OF JESUS
GODS FRIENDS
HEIRS
HOLY AND RIGHTEOUS ONES
KINGS
MASTERPIECES
MEMBERS OF ONE BODY
MINISTERS
MIRROR MIRROR ON THE WALL
NEW CREATURES
OVERCOMERS
PRIESTS
SAINTS
SATANS ADVERSARIES
SERVANTS
SPIRITUAL BEINGS
SUFFERERS
TEMPLES
WHO YOU ARE NOT GOD
WORSHIPERS

Made in the USA
Middletown, DE
16 August 2019